HEALING FLOWS

The River of Healing is Flowing ~It's Time to Step In

Timothy H. Linn

Copyright © 2025 Timothy H. Linn

HEALING FLOWS

All Rights reserved.

Unless otherwise indicated, all Scripture quotations are taken from the Holy Bible. Scriptures marked (AMP) are taken from the Amplified Bible. Copyright © 1954, 1958, 1962, 1964, 1965, 1987, 2015 by The Lockman Foundation.

Scripture quotations marked (TPT) are taken from The Passion Translation Bible®. Copyright © 2017, 2018 by Passion & Fire Ministries, Inc.

No part of this publication may be reproduced, stored in a retrieval system, or transmitted in any form or by any means without the prior permission of the author.

Table of Contents

Dedication 6

Introduction 8

Chapter 1 12
The Unchanging Nature Of God And His Will To Heal 12

Chapter 2 18
The Finished Work Of The Cross 18

Chapter 3 24
The Ministry Of Holy Spirit 24

Chapter 4 30
Faith – The Bridge Between Heaven And Earth 30

Chapter 5 36
Biblical Foundations For Laying On Of Hands 36

Chapter 6 42
Impartation And The Flow Of The Anointing 42

Chapter 7 48
Practical Activation – Stepping Out In Boldness............ 48

Chapter 8 54
Discerning The Spirit And The Need 54

Chapter 9 60
Miracles, Instant Healings, And Process Healings 60

Chapter 10 66
When Nothing Seems To Happen 66

Chapter 11 72
Healing Is Ours – Receiving By Faith 72

Chapter 12 78
Identity In Christ And Healing 78

Chapter 13 84
Dealing With Doubt, Fear, And Delay 84

Chapter 14 90
Healing Through Intimacy And Relationship 90

Chapter 15 96
Healing In The Soul And Body 96

Chapter 16..102
Practical Pathways To Receive 102

Chapter 17..108
Ministering While Needing Healing.....................................108

Chapter 18..114
Overflow – Healing Others From A Healed Identity ..114

Chapter 19..120
Community And Healing..120

Chapter 20..126
Living A Lifestyle Of Healing...126

Conclusion 132
Call To Salvation 134
Scripture Index... 135
Epilogue 141
Blessing.. 141
About The Author 143

Healing Flows

Dedication

To my amazing wife, Tahna René Linn, this book would not exist without you. From the very beginning, you have been a steady, radiant light—strong, gracious, and full of faith. You've encouraged me in ways I can never fully describe. And so often, I know you didn't realize the impact you were having. In moments when I felt stuck or unsure of myself—when life felt too weighty, the truth too vast, or my journey too incomplete—you were there. You believed in me. You spoke life into me. You reminded me of who I am and of the One who called me.

There were days when your quiet confidence in God's healing power gave me strength I couldn't find in myself. And then there were days when your fierce love and loyalty reminded me that I wasn't walking alone. You have always walked with me—not just beside me, but with purpose, with insight, and with a deep well of grace for me. In both your words and your silence, unknowingly, you helped me pull this message out of my heart and into these pages.

You have lived the life of silent testimony to me. You have carried the truth. You have been the living proof that faith works even when the journey is long. And you have given me room to grow, space to wrestle, and courage to continue on this path.

So much of what is written here was first lived in our conversations, in our prayers, and in the quiet places of my heart that only you and God know about. That's why I dedicate this book to you.

Thank you for being my encourager, my steady place, and my greatest blessing. Thank you for loving me through the process and calling me forward when I wanted to pull back. And thank you for being my strength when I had none. I am forever grateful to walk this life with you.

With all my love,

Introduction

To all who read these pages, please know, I didn't write this book as someone who's figured it all out. I wrote it as someone who believes—with every fiber of my being—that healing is part of the inheritance Jesus gave us, and yet who still needs to be reminded of it often. These pages are not coming from a place of perfection, but from pursuit. A pursuit of truth. A pursuit of Jesus. A pursuit of wholeness—not just for myself, but for others too.

Healing isn't just a doctrine I believe in. It's a reality I've seen with my own eyes. I've watched pain leave, nerves restore, movement return. I've seen God touch people in the most unexpected places—in churches, on sidewalks, in hardware stores, and in living rooms. I've felt the power of God flow through my hands while, at the same time, contending for healing in my own body. That tension is real. And it's holy.

This book was born in that place—in the in-between. In the stretching. In the moments when I had to decide again: Will I believe God's Word, even when my body doesn't line up yet? Will I keep laying hands on others, even when I'm still walking through my own healing journey? Will I keep saying yes?

The answer, for me, is yes. Over and over again, yes.

Healing Flows is not just a manual. It's a conversation. It's me sitting across the table from you saying, "This is real. This is for today. And this is for you." It's about giving and receiving healing—not as a formula, but as a lifestyle. Not from striving, but from identity. Not for the elite, but for the everyday believer.

There's more available in Christ than most of us are currently walking in. Healing is just one part of what Jesus purchased—but it's a part we cannot afford to ignore. My prayer is that as you read these chapters, Holy Spirit would ignite something in you—not only to receive healing but to become someone who carries it, who releases it, and who lives it out daily.

This book is written with Scripture, with stories, and with the honest conviction that Jesus still heals. That He still uses people—imperfect, in-process people—to do it. And that if you'll lean in, believe His Word, and obey His whispers, healing will flow through your life too. Let's step into it together.

My Disclosure Before We Start:

I want to let you know that I am not in any type of formal ministry. I'm not on staff at a church. I don't stand behind a pulpit. But I am someone who deeply believes in Jesus' command to "heal the sick, raise the dead, cleanse the leper, and cast out demons." I'm someone who's simply trying to live out what it means to follow Him—not just in belief, but in action.

When I mention "ministry" throughout these chapters, I'm not referring to a title or a platform. I'm talking about those everyday moments—when I reach out to someone in pain, when I pray for healing, when I lay hands in obedience and trust God to do what only He can do. That's what ministry means to me. It's the pursuit of bringing God's love and power into people's lives, one encounter at a time.

Healing Flows

CHAPTER 01

THE UNCHANGING NATURE OF GOD AND HIS WILL TO HEAL

Let's begin at the beginning—not just in terms of theology, but in terms of God's heart. If we're going to talk about healing, we have to first settle the question: *Is it really God's will to heal?* Because if we're not sure about that, faith can never fully take root.

But here's the good news: God hasn't changed. His nature has never shifted, and His heart toward you is steady, strong, and full of compassion. Malachi 3:6 says, "I am the Lord, I do not change." Hebrews 13:8 echoes that truth: "Jesus Christ is [eternally changeless, always] the same yesterday and today and forever" (AMP). If He healed then, He heals now.

Sometimes people will say, "Well, God *can* heal, but that doesn't mean He *will* heal." But that's not what we see in Scripture. We don't see Jesus walking around saying, "It's not the right time," or "Maybe later," or "This sickness is teaching you something." In fact, we see the opposite. Over and over again, Jesus responds to sickness with healing—not hesitation.

In Matthew 8, a man with leprosy comes to Jesus and says, "Lord, if You are willing, You can make me clean." What he was really asking is the same thing many of us ask deep down: "Are You willing?" And without flinching, Jesus reached out, touched him, and said, "I am willing. Be healed!" (Matthew 8:3 TPT). That one phrase—*I am willing*—should echo in our hearts forever.

Jesus is perfect theology. He said He only did what He saw the Father doing (John 5:19), so when Jesus healed, He revealed the will of God in action. He never once said, "I can't heal you right now because the Father is teaching you something through this." He didn't tell people to wait or to suffer through it a little longer. Every time healing was needed, compassion moved Him, and power flowed from Him.

Let's back up even further. In the Old Testament, God reveals Himself by His names—and one of those names is Jehovah Rapha, "the Lord who heals you" (Exodus 15:26). Healing isn't just something God does—it's who He is. That name is His covenant identity. And guess what? He doesn't change.

Psalm 103:2–3 reminds us: "Bless the Lord, O my soul, and forget not all His benefits—Who forgives all your sins, Who heals all your diseases" (AMP). Not some of them. *All* of them. Forgiveness and healing are side by side, flowing from the same covenant love.

And here's something powerful to consider: when God brought the Israelites out of Egypt, Psalm 105:37 says, "There was not one feeble among His tribes" (NKJV). Millions of people—men, women, children, slaves, elders—and *not one feeble one* among them. That's healing on a national level.

God didn't just want to set them free from bondage—He wanted them whole, body and soul.

Fast forward to the ministry of Jesus, and we see the same heart. "And He healed *all* who were sick. This fulfilled the word of the Lord through the prophet Isaiah, who said, 'He took our sicknesses and removed our diseases'" (Matthew 8:16–17 NLT). The ministry of healing wasn't a side gig for Jesus—it was the outworking of His compassion and His mission to destroy the works of the devil (1 John 3:8).

Still, many of us struggle with this question because of what we've seen—or haven't seen. Maybe we've prayed and not seen results. Maybe we've watched people suffer. Maybe we've experienced delay or disappointment ourselves. But we can't let experience redefine truth. God's Word is truth. Jesus is truth. And He is the Healer.

It's okay to bring those questions to God. He's not intimidated by our wrestle. But if we let our theology be shaped by pain instead of Scripture, we'll never walk in the full inheritance Jesus died to give us.

We have to come back to the Word and let it be the final authority. We can say, "I don't understand everything, but I trust You, God. I trust that You are good, and that You are still Jehovah Rapha." Healing is not a mystery to be solved—it's a gift to be received by faith.

And this is really key: God's desire to heal didn't change with the New Testament. It didn't diminish after the apostles. The same Spirit that raised Jesus from the dead lives in us (Romans 8:11), and He's still releasing resurrection power today. The book of Acts is still being written in the lives of believers who say yes to His call.

You don't have to wonder if He wants to heal you. You don't have to guess whether He's willing. Jesus already settled that forever on the cross. Healing was purchased right alongside forgiveness. Isaiah 53:5 (AMP) says, "He was wounded for our transgressions… and by His stripes we are healed." *Not might be. Not sometimes. Healed. *

Healing flows from His unchanging heart. From Genesis to Revelation, from the garden to the upper room, from the cross to your living room—God's desire is to restore, renew, and make whole. Always.

Declaration

Jesus, You are the same yesterday, today, and forever. You are my Healer, and You never change. I declare that it is Your will to heal, and I receive that truth deep in my spirit. I reject every lie that says You're distant, hesitant, or unwilling. I trust Your Word above my feelings. I choose to believe that You are Jehovah Rapha—the Lord who heals me—and You always will be.

Prayer

Father, thank You that You are good, and that Your will is healing. Thank You for revealing Your heart through Jesus, who healed all who came to Him. I come to You now, not based on my works, but based on Your Word and Your unchanging nature. Let the truth of Your will to heal saturate every part of my thinking. Holy Spirit, teach me to rest in the confidence that You are always for my wholeness. In Jesus' name, amen.

Healing Flows

CHAPTER 02

THE FINISHED WORK OF THE CROSS

There was a moment in history that changed everything. A moment when heaven roared, the veil was torn, and the power of sin, sickness, and separation was crushed under the weight of love. That moment was the cross.

When Jesus laid down His life, He wasn't only purchasing forgiveness for our sins. He was destroying the works of the devil—including sickness. Healing was included in the atonement. It wasn't an afterthought or an added bonus. It was a central part of why Jesus came.

Isaiah 53 gives us a prophetic glimpse into what Jesus carried for us. Verses 4–5 in the Amplified Bible say, "But [in fact] He has borne our griefs, and He has carried our sorrows and pains; yet we [ignorantly] assumed that He was stricken, struck down by God and degraded and humiliated [by Him]. But He was wounded for our transgressions, He was crushed for our wickedness [our sin, our injustice, our wrongdoing]; the punishment [required] for our well-being fell on Him, and by His stripes (wounds) we are healed."

Let that sink in for a moment. Jesus didn't just bear your sin. He bore your sickness. He carried your pain. The Hebrew words for "griefs" and "sorrows" in that verse literally translate to "sicknesses" and "pains." And He didn't do it halfway. He didn't carry them in theory—He absorbed them in His body, fully and completely. He took what was ours so that we could receive what was His.

Matthew 8 confirms that Jesus fulfilled Isaiah's prophecy during His earthly ministry. It says, "That evening, the people brought to Him many who were demonized. And by Jesus only speaking a word of healing over them, they were totally set free from their torment, and everyone who was sick received their healing! In doing this, Jesus fulfilled the prophecy of Isaiah: He put upon Himself our weaknesses, and He carried away our diseases" (Matthew 8:16–17 TPT).

Healing wasn't a side project. It was central to Jesus' mission. Every time He healed, He was demonstrating the kingdom. Every miracle was a shout from heaven: "This is what I came to do!" And when He went to the cross, He finished what He started. He bore the weight of it all—sin, shame, sickness, and death—and declared, "It is finished."

The Greek word for salvation in the New Testament is sozo. It means to save, heal, deliver, and make whole. It's a full package. When we say, "Jesus saves," we're also saying, "Jesus heals." He didn't separate those things at Calvary, and we shouldn't separate them now.

This is where so many of us get stuck. We believe Jesus can heal. We might even believe He wants to. But when symptoms linger or circumstances get loud, we start wondering if we've missed something. Maybe we didn't pray enough. Maybe our faith isn't strong enough. Maybe God is teaching us something. But friend, here's the truth: healing is not about our performance. It's about His finished work.

Colossians 2:14–15 (AMP) says, "Having canceled out the certificate of debt consisting of legal demands [which were in force] against us and which were hostile to us—and this certificate He has set aside and completely removed by nailing it to the cross. When He had disarmed the rulers and authorities [those supernatural forces of evil operating against us], He made a public example of them [exhibiting them as captives in His triumphal procession], having triumphed over them through the cross."

Jesus didn't just deal with our sin. He stripped the enemy of every legal right to afflict us. The cross wasn't partial victory. It was total triumph. And healing is a manifestation of that triumph here and now. 1 Peter 2:24 (AMP) says, "He personally carried our sins in His body on the cross [willingly offering Himself on it, as on an altar of sacrifice], so that we might die to sin [becoming immune from the penalty and power of sin] and live for righteousness; for by His wounds you [who believe] have been healed."

Did you catch that? Have been healed. It's not just a promise for the future. It's a finished work we step into now by faith. Healing is not a possibility to pursue—it's a reality to receive. And that's the key: receiving. Not striving. Not begging. Not trying to earn something Jesus already gave. We don't have to convince God to heal us. We have to convince our hearts that He already has. Faith doesn't make God move—faith moves us into alignment with what's already done. It's like walking into a room that's already full of light. We don't need to ask for the sun to shine—we just need to open the blinds. The light is already there. Healing is already flowing from the cross. The more we see it, the more we believe it, the more we receive it.

But what if you're still waiting? What if healing hasn't shown up in your body yet? What if the pain is still real? Then let the cross be your anchor. Let the finished work be your foundation. Don't measure God's will by your experience—measure your experience by what Jesus already accomplished. When storms hit and questions swirl, go back to the place where healing was secured forever. Go back to the cross. Jesus didn't just forgive your sins—He bore your sickness. He didn't just promise you heaven—He made healing part of your inheritance now. He didn't say, "Someday you might be free." He said, "It is finished."

So lift your eyes. Set your heart on what He has done. Healing isn't on the way—it's already been delivered. And it's yours to receive.

Declaration

Jesus, I believe that You finished the work on the cross. You carried my sin, my sickness, and my pain. You bore every affliction so I could be healed and whole. I declare that I receive what You paid for. I don't have to earn it, I just have to believe. Thank You that healing is part of my salvation, and that by Your wounds, I have been healed.

Prayer

Father, thank You for the finished work of Jesus. Thank You that healing was secured at the cross and that I don't have to wonder if it's Your will. Let this truth go deep into my spirit. I choose to believe what You say over what I feel. I rest in the completeness of what Jesus has done. Holy Spirit, help me live from this place of victory and guide me into the fullness of all that Jesus purchased for me. In His mighty name I pray, amen.

Healing Flows

CHAPTER 03

THE MINISTRY OF HOLY SPIRIT

If you've ever wondered how healing actually happens—how the power of God moves through one human life to touch another—it all comes down to one thing: Holy Spirit.

Holy Spirit isn't just a force, a symbol, or a concept. He's a Person. He is God with us and in us, the same Spirit that hovered over the waters at creation and raised Jesus from the dead. He didn't retire after Pentecost or take a step back after the apostles passed on. He's just as present, just as powerful, and just as eager to move today as He was in the upper room.

When we talk about healing, we're really talking about the overflow of Holy Spirit's presence. Holy Spirit is the One who makes the finished work of the cross real and active in our lives. He takes what Jesus purchased and distributes it into our bodies, our minds, our spirits. Healing flows from the cross through the channel of the Spirit. Acts 10:38 says it plainly: "How God anointed Jesus of Nazareth with Holy Spirit and with great power; and He went around doing good and healing all who were oppressed by the devil, because God was with Him" (AMP). Even Jesus—fully God and fully man—ministered healing through the anointing of Holy Spirit. If the Son of God relied on the Spirit to release healing, how much more do we?

And the beautiful part is this: that same Spirit now lives inside every believer. Romans 8:11 (AMP) says, "And if the Spirit of Him who raised Jesus from the dead lives in you, He who raised Christ Jesus from the dead will also give life to your mortal bodies through His Spirit who lives in you." This isn't a poetic metaphor. It's a practical promise. The life-giving power of God is dwelling in you right now, and it's available to bring healing—not just to you, but through you.

When Holy Spirit fills a life, healing becomes personal. He doesn't just release power—He brings presence. He whispers truth in our innermost places. He leads us to the right Scripture at the right time. He fills us with boldness when we feel weak. He opens our spiritual eyes to see what God is doing and partners with us to release it.

I remember a season that changed everything for me. I had been ministering healing to others for some time—praying for people in faith, seeing breakthroughs, watching God move in beautiful, unexpected ways. And then came the diagnosis.

Spinal cord compression. A slow, creeping threat that could end in paralysis. The symptoms were real. The reports were serious. There were days when it felt like my whole body was betraying me, and yet... there was this whisper in my spirit that wouldn't let go: "Heal the sick." It was as if Holy Spirit was saying, "Don't stop. Keep going. I'm still in you. I still want to move through you." So I kept ministering. I'd lay hands on others even while I was hurting. I prayed for people with back problems, nerve pain, slipped discs, and I watched as God healed them—right in front of me. One person's nerve damage disappeared. Another's chronic back pain instantly lifted. Over and over again, I saw Holy Spirit touch people's lives through mine, even as I was waiting for my own healing to fully manifest. Eventually, I underwent surgery. I'm still on the journey of full recovery. But here's the incredible thing: healing never stopped flowing. Because Holy Spirit never left.

That's the kind of God we serve. He's not limited by what we feel. He doesn't wait until we're completely healed to start moving through us. He simply looks for vessels—yielded, trusting, available. His power isn't hindered by our process. In fact, He loves to work through us in the middle of our process, because that's when we learn to lean on Him the most.

John 14:16–17 (AMP) says, "And I will ask the Father, and He will give you another Helper (Comforter, Advocate, Intercessor, — Counselor, Strengthener, Standby), to be with you forever—the Spirit of Truth, whom the world cannot receive... but you know Him because He (the Holy Spirit) remains with you continually and will be in you." He is your Helper. Not just when you feel strong, but especially when you feel weak. He's not waiting for you to get it all together. He's already in you, already working, already stirring healing inside of you and flowing healing through you to others.

Sometimes people ask, "Can I really pray for someone else's healing if I haven't received mine yet?" The answer is a resounding yes. The power doesn't come from you. It comes from Him. You're not the healer. You're the carrier. And as long as you're willing, Holy Spirit is ready.

It's in those moments—those raw, real, imperfect moments—when we say, "Lord, I trust You anyway," that healing flows the most freely. Not because we've earned it, but because we're yielded. Because we're leaning on the Spirit, not on our own strength.

Holy Spirit delights to glorify Jesus. And one of the most powerful ways He does that is through healing. It points to the cross. It confirms the Gospel. It reveals the love of the Father. And He's still doing it today—through people just like you and me.

Declaration

Holy Spirit, You live in me. You are my Strengthener, my Helper, my Healer, and my Guide. I declare that I am not alone in this journey. I yield to Your power. I trust that You are still healing today—both in me and through me. I choose to believe that You can flow through my life, even in my weakness. I am a vessel of healing, filled with the Spirit of the Living God.

Prayer

Precious Holy Spirit, thank You for abiding in me. Thank You for never leaving, even in my moments of pain, doubt, or weakness. Teach me to listen to Your voice. Help me to walk with You in greater intimacy. Use my life to glorify Jesus. Let healing flow from within me—into my body, my soul, and the lives of those around me. I give You full permission to move. Be glorified in and through me. In Jesus' name, amen.

Healing Flows

CHAPTER 04

FAITH – THE BRIDGE BETWEEN HEAVEN AND EARTH

Faith isn't just a topic we learn about—it's a reality we live from. If grace is God's supply, then faith is our connection point. It's the bridge between what God has already provided through the cross and what we experience here on earth. Without it, we stand on the edge of promise but never enter in. With it, we step into the fullness of everything Jesus paid for—including healing.

But faith can feel mysterious sometimes, can't it? We hear so much about it, yet many believers silently wonder, "Do I have enough faith? Am I doing it right? Why hasn't healing shown up yet if I believe?" These are honest questions—and the good news is, the Word doesn't leave them unanswered.

Hebrews 11:1 (TPT) gives us this definition: "Now faith brings our hopes into reality and becomes the foundation needed to acquire the things we long for. It is all the evidence required to prove what is still unseen." Faith brings heaven's reality into our present moment. It's the evidence that even before we see the healing, it's already ours.

Faith isn't pretending the pain doesn't exist. It's refusing to let the pain have the final word. Faith isn't about hype or emotion. It's about confidence—confidence in the goodness of God, the power of His Word, and the finished work of the cross.

Romans 10:17 (AMP) says, "So faith comes from hearing [what is told], and what is heard comes by the [preaching of the] message concerning Christ." If you're feeling weak in faith, the best thing you can do is immerse yourself in the truth of God's Word. Faith doesn't grow through effort. It grows through exposure. When we keep hearing the truth of who God is and what Jesus has done, our hearts begin to believe it.

And believing is where the miracle happens.

One of the clearest examples of faith in action is the woman with the issue of blood in Mark 5. She had suffered for twelve years. Every doctor had failed her. She was out of options. But then she heard about Jesus. And when she heard, something awakened inside of her. She said to herself, "If I just touch His clothing, I will get well." (Mark 5:28 AMP).

That was faith speaking. Not wishful thinking. Not desperation. Faith. And she didn't just believe—she acted. She pressed through the crowd, reached out, and touched Him. Immediately, the bleeding stopped. And Jesus knew power had gone out from Him. When she confessed what she had done, Jesus didn't rebuke her. He didn't say, "It was My power that did it." He said, "Daughter, your faith [your personal trust and confidence in Me] has restored you to health. Go in peace and be [permanently] healed from your suffering" (Mark 5:34 AMP).

Faith connects us to power. Her faith didn't *earn* healing—it *received* it. And that's the difference. Faith is never about making God do something. It's about receiving what He's already freely given.

Ephesians 2:8 (AMP) says, "For it is by grace [God's remarkable compassion and favor drawing you to Christ] that you have been saved [actually delivered from judgment and given eternal life] through faith. And this [salvation] is not of yourselves [not through your own effort], but it is the [undeserved, gracious] gift of God." Healing flows the same way—by grace through faith.

And here's something to remember: faith can be both for receiving *and* for giving. Sometimes, we have faith to be healed. Other times, we have faith to minister healing to others. Both are beautiful. Both are scriptural. But they require different postures of the heart.

Faith to receive is about trust—trusting that God has already done it, that it belongs to you, that you don't need to strive. It often looks like resting, confessing, thanking, and standing on His Word when nothing seems to change.

Faith to give, on the other hand, is bold. It steps out. It lays hands. It speaks to pain and commands it to leave. It looks like Jesus in Matthew 10:8 when He said, "Heal the sick, raise the dead, cleanse the lepers, cast out demons. Freely you have received, freely give" (AMP). You don't wait until you feel perfectly qualified or healed yourself—you act because Jesus said to, and you trust Holy Spirit to move.

The enemy loves to whisper lies here. "Who are you to pray for healing? You're still waiting for yours." But faith shuts those lies down. Faith says, "God can use me, even in process. The Healer lives in me." Remember, you're not releasing your perfection—you're releasing His power.

James 5:15 (AMP) declares, "The prayer of faith will restore the one who is sick, and the Lord will raise him up." This is a promise. Not a possibility. The Lord honors faith-filled prayers—not because He's distant, but because He loves it when we agree with Him.

And when it gets hard—when the waiting stretches longer than expected—faith still stands. Ephesians 6:13 (AMP) tells us, "Therefore, put on the complete armor of God… and having done everything [that the crisis demands], to stand firm [in your place, fully prepared, immovable, victorious]."

Sometimes standing *is* faith. Choosing not to give up *is* faith. Praising when nothing changes *is* faith. And I promise you, God sees it. He honors it. He responds to it.

You don't need to have perfect faith. You just need to believe Him. Even mustard seed faith is powerful—because the strength of your faith isn't in its size, it's in its object. And when your faith is in Jesus, you can move mountains.

Declaration

Jesus, I believe You. I believe Your Word is true, and Your promises are mine. I declare that by grace, through faith, I receive the healing You purchased for me. I will not be moved by symptoms or circumstances—I am anchored in truth. I am filled with boldness to pray for others and to receive for myself. Faith lives in me, and healing flows through me.

Prayer

Father, thank You for the gift of faith. Teach me to walk by faith and not by sight. I choose to trust You more than I trust my feelings. Let Your Word fill my heart and renew my mind. Holy Spirit, help me grow in boldness—both to receive healing and to release it. Thank You that my faith is not in my own efforts, but in Your finished work. I receive all that You have for me, and I declare Your goodness over my life. In Jesus' name, amen.

Healing Flows

CHAPTER 05

BIBLICAL FOUNDATIONS FOR LAYING ON OF HANDS

There's something deeply powerful about touch—especially when it's filled with faith and led by Holy Spirit. In Scripture, one of the primary ways healing flowed was through the laying on of hands. It wasn't a ritual or tradition. It was a divine point of contact where heaven met earth—where the anointing transferred and the sick were made well.

This practice runs through the entire storyline of Scripture. In the Old Testament, laying on of hands was used to bless, to commission, and to transfer something spiritually significant. But in the New Testament, it becomes even more dynamic. Through Jesus and the early church, it became one of the primary ways healing, anointing, and impartation flowed.

Jesus could have healed with just a word—and often did—but He also chose to touch. Why? Because He's not a distant Savior. He's personal. He's a hands-on Healer. And through the laying on of hands, He reveals the tenderness of the Father's heart.

Luke 4:40 (AMP) says, "While the sun was setting [marking the end of the sabbath day], all those who had any who were sick with various diseases brought them to Him; and laying His hands on each one [of them], He was healing them..." Every single person. He didn't rush. He didn't skip a few. He laid hands on *each one*, and healing flowed.

Mark 6:5 (AMP) tells us that in His own hometown, "He could not do a miracle there at all [because of their unbelief], except that He laid His hands on a few sick people and healed them." Even in the atmosphere of doubt, the laying on of hands carried enough faith and power to break through and heal. This was not a symbolic act. It was a Spirit-filled impartation.

The early church continued this practice faithfully. When Ananias laid his hands on Saul in Acts 9:17–18 (AMP), it says, "He laid his hands on Saul, and said, 'Brother Saul, the Lord Jesus… has sent me so that you may regain your sight and be filled with Holy Spirit.' Immediately, something like scales fell from Saul's eyes, and he regained his sight." Healing. Impartation. Holy Spirit power—all released through one act of obedience.

Later, Paul writes to Timothy and reminds him of the moment that changed his life: "I'm writing to encourage you to fan into a flame and rekindle the fire of the spiritual gift God imparted to you when I laid my hands upon you" (2 Timothy 1:6 TPT). Even spiritual gifts and callings were stirred and activated through this same method.

But this isn't just something for Jesus and the apostles. It's for *all who believe*. Mark 16:17–18 (AMP) makes it clear: "These signs will accompany those who have believed… they will lay hands on the sick, and they will get well." That's your inheritance. That's your call. You don't have to be a pastor or have a ministry title. You just have to believe. When you lay your hands on someone in faith, Holy Spirit is ready to move. It doesn't depend on your emotions or eloquence—it depends on His presence.

I remember one moment that still leaves me in awe. I was praying for my buddy's rotator cuff. His shoulder was in a lot of pain and had limited movement. As I ministered healing to his shoulder, the pain began to lessen and his range of motion increased dramatically. But then something unexpected happened—something we hadn't even been praying for. He suddenly felt a warmth in his knee, followed by a sense of release. Now, he hadn't mentioned his knee at all. But for years, it had been injured so badly that he couldn't ride his bike—something he loved to do. The condition had limited him for a long time. And in that one moment, while we were praying for something completely different, God touched his knee and healed it instantly. To this day—he's been riding his bike with no pain, no issues, and complete freedom. That wasn't my doing. That was the presence of God responding to a simple act of obedience: laying hands on a friend in faith and letting the power flow.

This is the beauty of how healing works. We may aim in one direction, but Holy Spirit knows exactly what's needed. The anointing isn't limited to our intention. It moves according to His heart. When you lay hands on someone, you are creating a point of contact for the presence of God to move. Healing doesn't come from your hands—but it flows through them. You're not the source, but you are the vessel. And God loves to use vessels who are willing to say yes, even when they don't feel qualified.

Jesus hasn't changed. He still touches. And now, He touches through you.

Declaration

Jesus, You said that those who believe will lay hands on the sick and see them recover. I believe. I receive that as my assignment. My hands are anointed because You live in me. When I lay hands on the sick, healing flows—not because of who I am, but because of who You are. I trust You to move through me with power.

Prayer

Father, thank You for the beautiful simplicity of laying on of hands. Thank You that I don't have to wait to feel ready—I just have to believe. Holy Spirit, give me eyes to see the hurting around me. Give me courage to reach out and touch, knowing You will do the rest. Let my hands be vessels of Your glory and compassion. I surrender them to You. Use them to bring healing, hope, and restoration. In Jesus' name, amen.

IMPARTATION AND THE FLOW OF THE ANOINTING

There's a divine mystery that every Spirit-filled believer gets to walk in—and it's this: the anointing of Holy Spirit doesn't just rest on us, it flows through us. When we lay hands on the sick, we're not hoping something might happen—we're releasing something that already lives within us. That's what impartation is. It's the transfer of something spiritual, something tangible, something holy, from one person to another by the Spirit of God.

This isn't about hype or charisma. It's not reserved for those with a title or a microphone. The anointing isn't something we earn—it's something we carry because of who lives inside of us. The moment you were born again, Holy Spirit took up residence in you. And when you were filled with His power, you were marked for impartation. You became a conduit of heaven.

Jesus made this clear. In John 7:38–39 (TPT), He said, "Believe in Me so that rivers of living water will burst out from within you, flowing from your innermost being just like the Scripture says!" And John explains, "Jesus was prophesying about Holy Spirit that believers were being prepared to receive." That river inside you—It's the anointing. It's the Spirit, and it flows.

The early church understood this. In Acts 8, Peter and John laid hands on new believers, and Holy Spirit was imparted. In Acts 19, Paul laid hands on twelve men in Ephesus, and they began to speak in tongues and prophesy. Power was released through physical contact, led by faith, and guided by the Spirit.

Impartation is never just mechanical. It's relational. It flows through intimacy with God and obedience to His prompting. When we lay hands on others, we're not transferring our greatness—we're releasing His presence. We are not the healer. We're the carrier. Paul wrote to the Romans, "I long to see you so that I may impart to you some spiritual gift to strengthen and establish you" (Romans 1:11 AMP). This wasn't manipulation or magic—this was a father in the faith, eager to see believers strengthened by the power of the Spirit that dwelled within him.

We don't talk about this enough, but the anointing is transferable. Elijah passed his mantle to Elisha. Jesus breathed on His disciples and said, "Receive Holy Spirit." The apostles laid hands on others and gifts were stirred, callings were confirmed, healing broke forth. Impartation is God's idea. He chooses to move through His people, not just to them.

Now, let's be clear—God doesn't need us to lay hands for Him to heal. He can move however He wants. But He chooses to partner with us. And the laying on of hands becomes a sacred act of agreement. We say with our bodies, "God is here. I believe He wants to move." And when we do that, The anointing flows.

A few years ago, my wife, Tahna, and I met a Christian couple at a friend's house in Evergreen, Colorado. We had gone there originally to minister healing to the husband, but during our time together, both he and his wife began to share something deeply personal—they had been saved for years, they loved Jesus, and they knew Holy Spirit lived in them, but neither of them had ever spoken in tongues. They had desired it for a long time, earnestly seeking their prayer language, but it had never come. We gently asked them if they would like us to lay hands on them and help activate what was already inside them. They both said yes with such hunger. They were excited, expectant, and ready. As the four of us began to pray together, we laid hands on them in faith, asking Holy Spirit to stir up the gift already deposited in them. And within just a few minutes, both of them began to speak in tongues. They started with the simple sounds that bubbled up in their spirits and mouths—hesitant at first, but growing with confidence as the Spirit gave utterance. It wasn't forced. It wasn't manufactured. It was already in them—just waiting to be released through faith and impartation. Today, they're both actively using their prayer language and growing in the Spirit. That moment marked a new chapter in their lives, and it will forever be in all four of our hearts.

This is what impartation looks like. It's not us giving people something we own—it's us helping them unlock what God has already given them. It's the Spirit flowing through us to stir, confirm, and activate what's been placed inside others.

Sometimes you'll feel it—a heat in your hands, a weight in the room, a surge of boldness you didn't expect. Other times, it may feel like nothing is happening. But the Spirit is always at work. You don't have to feel the anointing for it to flow. You just have to release it by faith.

Jesus gave us authority. In Luke 10:19 (AMP), He said, "Listen carefully: I have given you authority [that you now possess] to tread on serpents and scorpions, and [the ability to exercise authority] over all the power of the enemy (Satan); and nothing will [in any way] harm you." This authority isn't a badge we wear—it's a weapon we use. When you lay hands on someone, you're exercising that authority. You're commanding sickness to go. You're releasing healing to come. You're enforcing what Jesus already finished.

And here's something else: the anointing increases as we use it. The more we step out, the more we become aware of the Spirit's flow. We begin to recognize how He moves through us. We become more sensitive to His leading. And our confidence grows—not in ourselves, but in Him.

Impartation isn't about hype. It's not about being loud or dramatic. It's about being available. Holy Spirit doesn't need a stage. He just needs a vessel. And that vessel is you. You carry the anointing. You carry the life of God. And when you touch others in faith, heaven touches earth.

Declaration

Holy Spirit, thank You that You live in me. I declare that the same power that raised Jesus from the dead flows through me. I carry the anointing, and when I lay hands on the sick, You move. I do not minister from my own ability, but from Your endless supply. I am a vessel of impartation, and the flow of the Spirit increases in me daily.

Prayer

Father, thank You for choosing to move through Your children. Thank You that I am not empty—I am full of Your Spirit. Teach me to steward the anointing with reverence and boldness. Let me recognize Your flow and move when You prompt me. I don't want to hold back—I want to release everything You've placed inside me. Let healing, power, and freedom flow through my hands. In Jesus' name, amen.

Healing Flows

CHAPTER 07

PRACTICAL ACTIVATION – STEPPING OUT IN BOLDNESS

There comes a point when teaching must turn into practice, and revelation must lead to action. Healing wasn't meant to stay in the pages of Scripture—it was meant to flow through your hands into everyday life. That means at some point, you've got to step out. You've got to take the risk. You've got to believe that what Jesus said is true and act on it like it's true.

The good news is that this Boldness isn't a personality trait. It's the result of faith and love working together. It doesn't mean you'll never feel nervous. It just means you're more convinced of God's power than your own insecurity.

There's a story in Acts 3 that perfectly captures this moment of activation. Peter and John are walking to the temple and come across a man who's been crippled from birth. He's sitting at the gate called Beautiful, asking for money. But Peter looks him in the eye and says something bold, unfiltered, and full of fire: "Silver and gold I do not have, but what I do have I give to you: In the name of Jesus Christ the Nazarene—[begin now to] walk and go walking!" (Acts 3:6 AMP). Then Peter takes him by the hand and lifts him up. And instantly, the man's feet and ankles are strengthened. He jumps up, walks, and starts praising God in the middle of the temple. That's practical activation. Peter didn't stop and ask if he felt "led." He didn't ask Jesus to come down and do something. He simply recognized what he carried—the name, the authority, the Spirit—and he gave it away. And you carry that same power. That same Spirit. That same name.

Jesus didn't say, "Pray for Me to heal the sick." He said, "Heal the sick" (Matthew 10:8). That's an action verb. That's a commission. You've been authorized. But here's the reality: most people don't step out because they're afraid. Afraid of getting it wrong. Afraid nothing will happen. Afraid they'll look foolish. And let's be honest—that fear is real. I've felt it, too. I've had moments when my heart was racing, palms were sweating, and the internal dialogue was loud: What if this doesn't work? What if they don't get healed? What if I look like a fool? But in those moments, the question isn't, "What if nothing happens?" The real question is—"What if God does move?"

Love has to become louder than fear. Compassion must overpower hesitation. Because when your heart burns with the desire to see people free, you'll take the risk. You'll lay hands anyway. You'll speak life anyway. You'll step out—not because you're confident in yourself, but because you're confident in Him. And here's the beautiful thing: God loves to show up for those who take the risk. You don't have to start on a stage. You can start at your kitchen table. At the grocery store. In a parking lot. At your workplace. It doesn't have to be dramatic—it just has to be real. You see someone limping, offer to pray. Someone mentions chronic pain, ask if you can lay hands on their shoulder. You feel a nudge during worship, act on it. That's practical activation. You don't wait for the perfect moment—you become the moment God uses.

Don't be afraid of missing it. You learn as you go. Boldness grows with use. Every time you step out, your sensitivity sharpens. Your faith deepens. Your courage multiplies. And most importantly—people encounter Jesus. Paul said in 1 Corinthians 2:4–5 (AMP): "And my message and my preaching were not in persuasive words of wisdom [using clever rhetoric], but [they were delivered] in demonstration of the [Holy] Spirit [operating through me] and of [His]power [stirring the minds of the listeners and persuading them], so that your faith would not rest on the wisdom and rhetoric of men, but on the power of God." People don't need polished prayers—they need encounters. And boldness is what makes space for that.

Don't wait until you feel ready. Step out while you're trembling. That's when the anointing shows up. God loves to fill our weak yes with His strong presence. And don't be discouraged if the first person you pray for doesn't get healed. Keep going. Jesus prayed for a blind man in Mark 8, and the man said, "I see people... but they look like trees walking around." So Jesus prayed again. And the man's sight was fully restored.

Sometimes you'll need to pray twice. Sometimes the healing will come gradually. Sometimes you won't see immediate results. But faith presses on. Faith lays hands anyway. Your role is obedience. Obey, and see the miraculous!

So go for it. Take the risk. Activate what's already in you. And trust His finished work.

Declaration

Jesus, You have filled me with Your Spirit and authorized me to release healing. I declare that boldness is rising in me. I will not be silenced by fear or hesitation. I am a vessel of power and compassion. I will step out in faith, lay hands on the sick, and watch You move. I choose obedience over comfort and faith over fear.

Prayer

Father, I ask for boldness—not the boldness that comes from personality, but the kind that comes from knowing who You are in me. Let love silence fear. Let faith rise above doubt. I don't want to just hear the Word—I want to do it. Holy Spirit, prompt me, guide me, and empower me. Give me eyes to see the ones You want to touch and the courage to step out. I say yes. In Jesus' name, amen.

Healing Flows

CHAPTER 08

DISCERNING THE SPIRIT AND THE NEED

There's more to healing ministry than just laying hands and quoting a verse. Sometimes, the need is deeper than what we see on the outside. Sometimes what looks like a physical problem is actually rooted in emotional pain, trauma, or even spiritual oppression. And that's why we need discernment. Not just natural understanding—but spiritual sensitivity to Holy Spirit.

The truth is, healing ministry isn't just about power—it's about partnership. Holy Spirit is always speaking, always leading, always showing us how to love people well. And when we learn to minister healing in step with Him, the results go far beyond what we could accomplish on our own. Jesus modeled this beautifully. In John 5:19 (AMP), He said, "I assure you and most solemnly say to you, the Son can do nothing of Himself [of His own accord], unless it is something He sees the Father doing; for whatever things the Father does, the Son [in His turn] also does in the same way." Jesus—the Son of God—didn't act independently. He watched. He listened. He moved in sync with the Father through the Spirit.

In Luke 5:17–26, we see the story of the paralyzed man who was lowered through the roof. His friends were believing for a physical miracle. But the first thing Jesus said wasn't, "Be healed." It was, "Friend, your sins are forgiven." Why? Because Jesus discerned the real need first. Yes, He healed the man's body too—but He addressed the heart before the symptoms. This kind of discernment doesn't come from logic or reasoning—it comes from intimacy. The more time you spend with Holy Spirit, the more clearly you'll hear Him. He may show you a specific condition, a moment from someone's past, a word of knowledge, or simply a deep sense of love for the person in front of you. He knows what's really going on beneath the surface.

1 Corinthians 2:10–11 (AMP) says, "For God has unveiled them and revealed them to us through the [Holy] Spirit; for the Spirit searches all things [diligently], even [sounding and measuring] the profound depths of God... For what person knows the thoughts and motives of a man except the man's spirit within him? So also no one knows the thoughts of God except the Spirit of God." When you step into healing ministry, you don't have to figure people out—you just have to listen. The Spirit knows exactly what's going on in their heart, their history, and their body. And He's more than willing to tell you what you need to know in that moment.

Sometimes the need is obvious—a broken arm, a limp, a diagnosis. But other times, the physical condition is connected to something deeper. A wound in the soul. Years of fear. Bitterness. Trauma. Or, at times, spiritual oppression. And if we're not listening, we might miss the real doorway to healing.

I remember a time in Walsenburg, Colorado, when I was praying for a man who had severe sciatica pain. We were working through his discomfort and helping get his hips into alignment. The pain in his legs left, and physically he seemed to be improving—but something didn't sit quite right in my spirit during the physical healing. I felt anxious the whole time. As I started to walk away and look around the room for who to pray for next, I began to feel an intense, almost overwhelming anxiety. It wasn't normal. It hit me like a wave—nervousness, agitation, even to the point of almost shaking. And in that moment, I heard Holy Spirit say, "Pay attention." So I turned back and asked the man, "Do you often feel very uptight, nervous, and fidgety?" His wife, standing next to him, practically laughed out loud and said, "Oh yes, absolutely." He smiled and nodded, almost embarrassed, like I'd just read his mail.

That's when Holy Spirit revealed to me that what I was sensing wasn't just natural anxiety—it was a spiritual oppression. I was picking up on a spirit that had been afflicting him for a long time. Right there, I commanded the oppressive spirit to leave him and never return. I also prayed for his body—everything affected by that torment—to come back into divine order. Immediately, he felt relief. But what really marked me was the follow-up months later. I saw them again, and both he and his wife commented on how much he had changed since that day. He'd been set free—freed from a spirit that had been restricting him his whole life. That's the power of discernment.

That's why we don't want to rush. Healing isn't a performance. It's ministry. It's heart-to-heart. Spirit-to-spirit. Take the time to ask Him, "Holy Spirit, what's really going on here? What do You want to do in this moment? What does this person need from You—not just physically, but fully?"

Isaiah 11:2 (AMP) describes the Spirit of the Lord as "the Spirit of wisdom and understanding, the Spirit of counsel and strength, the Spirit of knowledge and of the reverential and obedient fear of the Lord." That same Spirit lives in you. He knows. And He speaks. Don't underestimate the power of quiet listening. Sometimes the most anointed thing you can do is pause and wait. Healing flows best when we follow Him step by step. And sometimes, the Spirit may lead you to do something unusual—like have someone take a prophetic action, speak forgiveness, or pray for someone else in their moment of need. These aren't formulas. They're responses to what the Spirit is saying.

Discernment doesn't always come with fireworks. It often comes with a whisper. But when you follow that whisper, lives are transformed.

You don't need to be a spiritual detective. You just need to be a friend of Holy Spirit. He'll show you what you need to see, when you need to see it.

Declaration

Holy Spirit, I trust Your voice. I declare that I am sensitive to Your leading. I do not minister from my own understanding—I follow You. I have ears to hear and eyes to see. I will not rush or assume. I will listen and respond in faith. I release healing with discernment and love, just like Jesus.

Prayer

Holy Spirit, I want to partner with You fully. Teach me to slow down and listen. Help me discern the real need in the people I minister to. Let my hands be guided by compassion and my heart be in step with Yours. Speak to me, lead me, and show me how to love well. I don't want to just see people healed—I want to see them whole. In Jesus' name, amen.

Healing Flows

MIRACLES, INSTANT HEALINGS, AND PROCESS HEALINGS

Healing doesn't always look the same. Sometimes it happens in an instant, like a sudden flash of lightning. Other times, it unfolds gradually, like a sunrise breaking over the horizon. But whether fast or slow, it's still the same Jesus. And the key to partnering with Him is learning to trust His ways—no matter how they show up.

Let's start with the miracles. Miracles are those moments when heaven invades earth with undeniable force. They're immediate, breathtaking, and impossible to miss. A tumor disappears. A deaf ear opens. Pain vanishes in an instant. One moment you're praying—and the next, it's done.

We see these moments all over the Gospels. In Matthew 8:3 (AMP), Jesus reaches out and touches a man with leprosy and says, "I am willing; be cleansed." And immediately his leprosy was cleansed. There was no delay. No process. Just the raw power of God at work.

I've seen it happen with my own eyes. I've ministered to people in all kinds of situations, but one moment I'll never forget was when I prayed for a longtime friend who had a serious back issue and was seriously contemplating surgery. I commanded every sickness, disease, harassing spirit, and pain to leave his body in the name of Jesus, and for his body to be healed. Immediately, he felt about 90% relief. I let him know that God finishes what He starts, "I am convinced and confident of this very thing, that He who has begun a good work in you will [continue to] perfect and complete it until the day of Christ Jesus [the time of His return]."— [Philippians 1:6, AMP] I placed my hand on his shoulder again—this time without saying a word. Within seconds, he heard a pop in his neck, and the rest of the pain vanished. He was completely healed. A problem he had struggled with for at least eight years was gone in under a minute. That's the power of Jesus.

Those moments are unforgettable. They build faith. They show off the goodness and compassion of Jesus in ways that leave people in tears of joy and wonder. And yes—we should expect them. We should eagerly desire the suddenly of God.

But what about when it's not instant? That's where process healings come in. These are the ones that unfold over time—sometimes hours, sometimes days, weeks, or even months. You pray, and something shifts—but the full breakthrough takes time. This doesn't make it any less divine. In fact, it often creates deeper intimacy and trust.

Mark 8:22–25 gives us a rare look at this kind of healing in Jesus' ministry. A blind man is brought to Him. Jesus spits on his eyes, lays hands on him, and then asks, "Do you see anything?" The man replies, "I see people, but they look like trees, walking around." So Jesus lays hands on him again—and this time, he sees clearly. Even Jesus ministered in layers. The first touch brought change. The second brought clarity. Process doesn't mean failure. It means persistence. It means

God is still working, and He invites us to keep pressing in. Hebrews 6:12 (AMP) tells us to "be imitators of those who through faith and by patient endurance [even when suffering] are [now] inheriting the promises." The promise is healing. But the path might look different than expected.

When we pray for others, it's important to help them recognize what God is doing—even in the small beginnings. "Has anything shifted?" "Is the pain reduced at all?" These aren't filler questions. They're ways to honor the process. To help people notice the flow of healing—even if it hasn't yet fully manifested.

Sometimes, healing begins in the spirit before it shows up in the body. It might start with peace. Or sleep. Or energy. Or a lifting of anxiety. Celebrate those things. They're signs that the power of God is moving.

We can't afford to box God in. He's not a formula. He's a Father. And sometimes, the process is about more than the condition—it's about the person. He's building trust. Renewing identity. Restoring hope. But let me say this clearly: process should never cause us to lower our expectation. We're not looking for a "maybe someday." We're contending for full healing every time. And we keep standing until it comes. Don't be discouraged if it doesn't happen instantly. Keep praying. Keep declaring. Keep laying hands. Miracles are beautiful, but so is persistence. Jesus honors faith that doesn't give up. And remember—what may seem like a process to us could still be supernatural. The person who recovers in a week after years of suffering has still encountered a miracle. The gradual healing is no less divine than the sudden one.

Your job isn't to determine the timeline. Your job is to obey, to believe, and to keep your heart open to every way God might choose to move.

Healing Flows

Declaration

Jesus, I trust You—whether healing comes in a moment or unfolds over time. I declare that miracles are normal in my life. I lay hands expecting instant breakthrough, but I also trust You in the process. I will not give up. I will not lower my faith. You are the same Healer in every circumstance, and I partner with You no matter how healing shows up.

Prayer

Father, thank You for the variety of ways You move. Thank You for sudden miracles that show Your power—and for process healings that deepen our trust. Teach me to walk in faith without frustration, to celebrate every sign of healing, and to never stop contending for wholeness. Let boldness rise in me as I pray for others, and let Your love be the foundation for everything I do. In Jesus' name, amen.

Healing Flows

CHAPTER 10

WHEN NOTHING SEEMS TO HAPPEN

You step out in faith. You lay hands on the sick. You declare healing in Jesus' name. And then... nothing. No visible change. No immediate relief. No miracle moment.

We've all been there. And if you haven't yet, you will. Because this journey of healing isn't a formula—it's a relationship. And relationships require trust, especially when immediate perceived outcomes don't line up with expectations.

These are the moments that test your heart. When you've done everything, you know to do, and the pain remains. When you pray bold prayers, and the person still limps away. When your heart is full of compassion, but the breakthrough doesn't come. These moments hurt. They're humbling. They shake us. But they don't disqualify us. And they certainly don't change God.

Let's be honest—this is where a lot of people pull back. They feel embarrassed, disillusioned, or discouraged. The enemy whispers, "You missed it. You don't have what it takes. Maybe God doesn't really heal." But none of that is true. God's character hasn't changed. His Word hasn't changed. The cross hasn't lost its power. And neither has the commission: "Lay hands on the sick, and they will get well" (Mark 16:18 AMP).

They will recover. It may not be instant. It may not look the way we hoped. But recovery is still the promise.

When nothing seems to happen, it's not time to retreat—it's time to press in deeper. It's time to return to the Word, to refocus our hearts on who God is, and to trust His nature over our experience. Hebrews 10:23 (AMP) reminds us, "Let us seize and hold tightly the confession of our hope without wavering, for He who promised is reliable and trustworthy and faithful [to His word]." That verse doesn't say, "Let us only confess when we see results." It says without wavering. Faith doesn't fold in disappointment. Faith keeps showing up.

There's a mystery to healing we don't fully understand. Paul didn't shy away from it. He left Trophimus sick in Miletus (2 Timothy 4:20). He told Timothy to drink a little wine for his stomach issues (1 Timothy 5:23). Yet this same Paul saw the lame walk, the dead rise, and entire cities transformed by the power of God. We don't stop ministering healing because we hit resistance. We keep going—because the power isn't in our personal ability, it's in the finished work of the cross. Our job is obedience. And sometimes, the fruit of your faith won't show up until later. I've had people I prayed for walk away seemingly unchanged, only to hear weeks later that their symptoms disappeared, their scan came back clean, or they woke up completely healed the next morning. A delayed manifestation doesn't mean a denied miracle. Remember, we don't minister healing for the results—we minister because of love. Love keeps showing up. Love keeps praying. Love keeps believing. Love doesn't walk away when things don't look perfect.

You're not failing when nothing seems to happen. You're planting seeds. And seeds take time. Galatians 6:9 (AMP) encourages us: "Let us not grow weary or become discouraged in doing good, for at the proper time we will reap, if we do not give in." Some breakthroughs come quickly. Others require a little more water, a little more time, a little more faithfulness. But the harvest will come.

One of the most powerful things you can do after praying for someone and seeing no immediate result is to keep your heart encouraged. Speak life over yourself. Declare God's truth. Refuse to let disappointment take root. And most importantly—don't make doctrine out of disappointment. If someone doesn't get healed right away, that doesn't mean healing isn't God's will. It doesn't mean the cross wasn't enough. It just means you're still in the battle. And the only way to lose that battle is to stop swinging.

Healing ministry takes grit. It takes boldness, yes—but it also takes resilience. It takes the kind of stubborn faith that says, "Even if I don't see it right now, I'm not backing down. I know who my God is. I know what Jesus paid for. I know what I carry. And I will keep laying hands. I will keep believing. I will keep going." Because here's the truth: when nothing seems to happen, something is still happening. The Spirit is still moving. Seeds are being planted. Faith is being built. Love is being shown. And God is always faithful.

Declaration

Jesus, I will not be moved by what I see. I believe Your Word above all else. When nothing seems to happen, I will not stop. I will keep showing up. I will keep praying. I will keep laying hands on the sick. You are the same yesterday, today, and forever. And I trust You completely.

Healing Flows

Prayer

Father, thank You for Your faithfulness—even when I don't see the results I long for. Strengthen my heart when I feel discouraged. Remind me that You are still working, even in the silence. I choose to trust You more than I trust what I see. I will not pull back—I will press in. Use me to release Your love and power, no matter what. In Jesus' name, amen.

Healing Flows

CHAPTER 11

HEALING IS OURS – RECEIVING BY FAITH

Healing isn't a reward for good behavior. It's not a mysterious blessing for the lucky few. It's not something we have to chase or strive for. It's an inheritance, A gift. It's a finished reality, bought with blood, secured by covenant, and offered freely by grace. And the way we take hold of it is Faith. Not performance. Not desperation. Not spiritual gymnastics. Just simple, childlike trust in what Jesus already did.

This chapter is about owning your healing. Not wishing. Not begging. Receiving.

Isaiah 53:5 (AMP) says, "But He was wounded for our transgressions, He was crushed for our wickedness [our sin, our injustice, our wrongdoing]; the punishment [required] for our well-being fell on Him, and by His (wounds) we are healed."

Healing isn't something you have to convince God to do. It's something He already accomplished. And faith is the hand that takes what grace has already given. So let me say this clearly: healing is already yours. If you are in Christ, then everything He paid for belongs to you—including wholeness in your body, soul, and spirit.

That's the power of the Gospel. Jesus didn't just take your sin—He took your sickness. He didn't just make a way for you to go to heaven. He brought heaven into your body here and now. So when you reach out in faith for healing, you're not trying to get God to move—you're aligning yourself with what's already done.

That alignment starts with your mind. Romans 12:2 (AMP) says, "And do not be conformed to this world [any longer with its superficial values and customs], but be transformed and progressively changed [as you mature spiritually] by the renewing of your mind, [focusing on godly values and ethical attitudes], so that you may prove [for yourselves] what the will of God is, that which is good and acceptable and perfect [in His plan and purpose for you]." If your mind still believes you're sick, broken, or disqualified, then even though healing belongs to you, you won't walk in it. But when your mind is renewed to the truth—when you see yourself as already healed, already whole, already free—that's when manifestation begins to take shape.

Faith speaks. Faith sees. Faith stands. Faith doesn't say, "I'll believe it when I feel it." Faith says, "I believe it because He said it—and my body is coming into agreement." That's why declarations are so powerful. When you speak the Word of God over your body, you are not pretending. You are prophesying. You are commanding your body to line up with the truth of heaven. You are partnering with the Spirit instead of your symptoms.

Let me give you an example of how this works in practice. There was a season in my life when I was battling symptoms that didn't make sense. I knew what the Word said. I had seen healing in others. But now I needed to walk it out for myself. I remember lying in bed one night, feeling discouraged. I whispered, "Jesus, I know You already paid for this. Help me receive it." And Holy Spirit gently whispered back, "Then speak like it's done."—So I did. I laid hands on my own body and began to declare: "Sickness, you have no place here. Jesus already bore you. By His wounds, I am healed. Body, you align with heaven. Every cell, every nerve, every system—come into divine order. I receive what belongs to me. I receive what Jesus paid for." Nothing changed right away. But I kept going. Day after day, moment by moment. I chose to believe. And slowly—then suddenly—breakthrough came. The illness left. Strength returned. Healing flowed. Not because I strived, but because I received.

Sometimes healing is instant. Sometimes it unfolds. But the access point is always the same: faith. Now, faith isn't the absence of struggle. It's not denial. It's not pretending symptoms don't exist. It's choosing to believe that Jesus' finished work is greater than what you're feeling. You can acknowledge the diagnosis without bowing to it. You can feel the pain without agreeing with it. You can experience delay without letting go of your inheritance. That's what receiving by faith looks like. You hold on. You declare. You rest. You refuse to quit.

James 1:6–7 (TPT) says, "Just make sure you ask empowered by confident faith without doubting that you will receive. For the ambivalent person believes one minute and doubts the next. Being undecided makes you become like the rough seas driven and tossed by the wind."

Receiving isn't begging. It's confidence. You are not trying to get healed. You are healed by the stripes of Jesus—and your body is catching up to the truth. And here's something beautiful: God meets us in our process. Even when our faith feels small, He's still faithful. Even when we wobble, His promise doesn't change. Healing is not fragile—it's rooted in a covenant sealed with blood.

So let this chapter be your turning point. No more hoping one day it'll happen. No more wondering if God wants to. No more living at the mercy of your symptoms. Stand up inside and say, "Healing is mine. I receive it now. I align with truth. I will walk it out by faith. And I will see the goodness of God in my body."

Declaration

Jesus, I believe that You already paid for my healing. I receive it by faith. I declare that by Your stripes, I am healed. My body is not the final authority—Your Word is. I speak life over every part of me. I am not trying to get healed—I am walking in what is already mine. I thank You that healing flows now.

Prayer

Father, thank You for the finished work of the cross. Thank You that healing is part of my inheritance. I choose to believe Your Word over my circumstances. I receive healing by faith, and I speak it over my body, mind, and soul. Holy Spirit, help me stand strong. Renew my mind. Strengthen my heart. Let every cell in my body come into divine alignment. I rest in what Jesus has done, and I thank You that I am whole. In Jesus' name, amen.

Healing Flows

CHAPTER 12

IDENTITY IN CHRIST AND HEALING

You are not your symptoms. You are not your diagnosis. You are not your pain, your trauma, or your history. You are a new creation in Christ, filled with His Spirit, sealed by His blood, and defined by His victory.

If the enemy can convince you otherwise—if he can get you to believe that sickness is your identity—he can keep you from walking in what's already yours. But when you know who you are? Healing becomes natural. It becomes normal. It becomes the overflow of your identity, not just a breakthrough you're trying to get. The starting place for healing isn't need—it's identity.

2 Corinthians 5:17 (AMP) says, "Therefore if anyone is in Christ [that is, grafted in, joined to Him by faith in Him as Savior], he is a new creature [reborn and renewed by Holy Spirit]; the old things [the previous moral and spiritual condition] have passed away. Behold, new things have come [because spiritual awakening brings a new life]." When you were born again, you didn't just get a ticket to heaven. You were completely remade. Your spirit was joined to Jesus. His righteousness became yours. His victory became yours. His life became yours. Galatians 2:20 (TPT) says, "My old identity

has been co-crucified with Messiah and no longer lives; for the nails of His cross crucified me with Him. And now the essence of this new life is no longer mine, for the Anointed One lives His life through me—we live in union as one!" That means sickness has no right to live in your body. Not because of how well you've behaved—but because of who now lives inside you. Healing flows from your identity in Christ, not your performance for Christ.

This truth changes everything. When you know you are healed in Him, you stop identifying with the issue. You stop saying, "my arthritis," "my condition," "my anxiety." Because those things are not yours—they were nailed to the cross with Jesus. You may be experiencing symptoms, but they are not your identity. They are trespassers. And you have authority to evict them. That authority is part of your new nature. As a child of God, you are seated with Christ in heavenly places (Ephesians 2:6). You're not begging for scraps from heaven's table. You're seated at the right hand of the Father, with the same Spirit that raised Jesus from the dead living inside of you.

Romans 8:11 (AMP) declares,

"And if the Spirit of Him who raised Jesus from the dead lives in you, He who raised Christ Jesus from the dead will also give life to your mortal bodies through His Spirit who lives in you." Not just eternal life—but resurrection life for your body. Right here. Right now. That means you don't need to strive to become something you're not. You simply need to agree with who you already are.

The enemy's greatest tactic is identity theft. He wants you to believe you're still sick, still bound, still struggling, still broken. But Jesus destroyed that narrative at the cross. You are not a sick person trying to get well. You are a healed person resisting sickness. And this shift in identity changes how you pray. You stop praying from desperation and start praying from victory. You stop seeing healing as a distant possibility and start seeing it as a present reality.

You begin to say:

"I am the healed of the Lord."

"Healing is not just something I believe in—it's who I am in Christ."

"My body is a temple of Holy Spirit, and every system must function in alignment with heaven."

And when symptoms show up, you don't panic. You don't cave. You don't agree. You speak from your identity.

You say:

"This isn't who I am. I'm not accepting this. In Jesus' name, you have to go."

I've seen this firsthand. There was a time I felt symptoms creeping back—familiar ones that I knew all too well. But instead of partnering with fear, I stood on truth. I said out loud, "That's not who I am anymore. I'm not hosting this. I'm not agreeing with this. Jesus already paid for my healing, and I'm walking in it." The symptoms left quickly. Not because I shouted loud, but because I stood firm. And that's what identity gives you—confidence. Confidence that the Word is true. Confidence that the Spirit lives in you. Confidence that the finished work of Jesus has become your new baseline.

Healing becomes part of your spiritual DNA. You don't chase it—you carry it. You may still be in process, but your identity is not up for negotiation. You are who God says you are. You are whole. You are redeemed. You are made new. And healing is already inside you, waiting to manifest. Walk in it. Speak it. Live it. It's already yours.

Declaration

I am not defined by my symptoms—I am defined by Christ. I am a new creation. I am the healed of the Lord. Sickness is not my identity. I walk in divine health because Jesus lives in me. His victory is my reality. I receive healing as part of who I am, not something I strive for.

Prayer

Father, thank You that I am a new creation in Christ. Thank You that healing is part of my identity. Help me to see myself the way You see me—whole, free, and filled with life. Holy Spirit, renew my mind with truth. Show me how to walk as a son, not a slave. I reject every label that doesn't come from You, and I receive the fullness of who I am in Jesus. Amen.

Healing Flows

CHAPTER 13

DEALING WITH DOUBT, FEAR, AND DELAY

There's something raw and real about the space between promise and manifestation. That in-between zone where you believe God's Word but the pain lingers. Where the healing hasn't shown up yet. Where you're declaring truth with your mouth but wrestling questions in your mind.

If you've ever felt the tension of believing while waiting, you're not alone. That space is sacred—it's where faith is forged. Doubt, fear, and delay are three of the most common battles people face when pursuing healing. They're not evidence of failure—they're opportunities for deeper intimacy with God and a stronger grip on His truth.

Doubt: The Whisper That Undermines Truth — Doubt says, "What if it's not really God's will?", "What if it's not working?", "What if I messed this up?". It's subtle. It often sounds reasonable. But doubt always attacks the integrity of God's Word.

James 1:6–8 (TPT) warns us, "Just make sure you ask empowered by confident faith without doubting that you will receive. For the ambivalent person believes one minute and doubts the next… When you are half-hearted and wavering it

Healing Flows

leaves you unstable. Can you really expect to receive anything from the Lord when you're in that condition?"

God isn't asking you to pretend doubt doesn't exist—He's inviting you to respond to it with truth. When doubt creeps in, you don't need to panic. You just need to anchor back to the Word. Declare what God has said louder than what your circumstances are saying.

Every time Jesus was tempted, He responded with, "It is written." You can do the same.

Say out loud:

"It is written—by His wounds I am healed."

"It is written—the prayer of faith will restore the sick."

"It is written—Jesus healed all who came to Him, and He never changes."

Fear: The Voice That Paralyzes Boldness. Fear tells you to back off. To stop praying. To settle. It exaggerates the symptoms and silences your authority. But fear is a liar. 2 Timothy 1:7 (AMP) says, "For God did not give us a spirit of timidity or cowardice or fear, but [He has given us a spirit] of power and of love and of sound judgment and personal discipline." Fear is not from God. It's a spirit—and you have authority over it.

Speak to it:

"Fear, you have no place in me. I refuse to bow to you. I am not afraid of delay. I am not afraid of pain. I am not afraid of what ifs. I trust my Father."

You don't need to feel brave to be bold. Faith isn't the absence of fear—it's the decision to act on truth anyway.

Delay: The Test of Endurance. This may be the hardest one—when you've prayed, believed, stood firm… and still nothing. Delay can be brutal. It tests your heart, stretches your faith, and presses against your endurance. But it's also where some of the most beautiful fruit is grown. Hebrews 10:35–36 (AMP) encourages us, "Do not, therefore, fling away your fearless confidence, for it has a glorious and great reward. For you have need of patient endurance [to bear up under difficult circumstances without compromising], so that when you have carried out the will of God, you may receive and enjoy to the full what is promised."

Delay is not denial. It's preparation. It's refining. It's a setup for something deeper than just a moment—it's about developing trust that holds firm in His finished work. And sometimes, healing isn't delayed at all—it's just happening in ways we can't yet see.

Let me remind you of this: Jesus didn't rebuke people for being in process. He met them there. He called Peter out onto the water while his faith was still maturing. He didn't wait until everything was perfect. He partnered with mustard-seed faith. So if you're walking through doubt, fear, or delay—don't condemn yourself. Just keep showing up. Keep speaking truth. Keep worshiping. Keep declaring healing. You're not alone in this. Holy Spirit is walking with you, strengthening you, encouraging you, reminding you of who you are and whose you are. You are not failing. You are growing.

Practical Tools for Pushing Through

- Daily Scripture Confession – Don't wait for feelings. Declare truth every day, out loud.

- Worship Instead of Worry – Turn on worship music. Praise Him before the breakthrough.

- Community Connection – Don't isolate. Stay connected with faith-filled believers.

- Journaling the Journey – Write down the small wins. Document any shift, peace, or whisper from God.

- Speak to Your Soul – Like David in Psalm 42, command your soul to hope in God.

Breakthrough is on the other side of persistence.

Declaration

I will not bow to doubt, fear, or delay. I trust in the faithfulness of my God. His Word is true, and His timing is perfect. I hold fast to the promise of healing, knowing that what Jesus paid for is already mine. I will not be moved by what I feel—I am anchored in truth.

Prayer

Father, You are faithful in every season. When I feel unsure, You are steady. When I feel afraid, You are near. When I see delay, You are still working. I choose to trust You. I cast out doubt. I reject fear. I hold onto Your Word. Let healing manifest in my body. And in the process, make me more like Jesus. Amen.

Healing Flows

CHAPTER 14

HEALING THROUGH INTIMACY AND RELATIONSHIP

Healing is not a transaction. It's not a spiritual vending machine where we press a button of faith and wait for a miracle. Healing flows from relationship. It comes from the heart of a Father who deeply loves His children. It flows from closeness, from communion, and from trust. When we make healing about performance or formulas, we reduce it to something mechanical. But healing—true, lasting, transformative healing—was always meant to flow from intimacy with God.

Psalm 103:2–3 (AMP) says, "Bless and affectionately praise the Lord, O my soul, and do not forget any of His benefits; Who forgives all your sins, Who heals all your diseases." Do you see the connection? Forgiveness. Healing. Restoration. These are the benefits of walking in relationship with Him. Healing isn't an isolated blessing—it's part of the full package of being united with Christ. When we know who He is and stay close to His heart, we begin to live in the flow of everything He's provided.

There's a moment in Luke 8 that perfectly captures this. A woman with an issue of blood reaches out in desperation and touches the hem of Jesus' garment. Instantly, her body is healed. But Jesus doesn't let the moment end there. He turns around and says, "Who touched Me?" Not because He didn't know, but because He wanted her to experience more than healing—He wanted her to experience connection. He called her out, not to embarrass her, but to affirm her. "Beloved daughter, your faith in Me released your healing. You may go with My peace." (Luke 8:48, TPT). In calling her daughter, He gave her identity. In giving her peace, He healed her soul. That's the heart of Jesus. He doesn't just fix bodies—He restores hearts.

Healing becomes personal when we slow down long enough to recognize that Jesus is not just our Healer—He is our friend, our Savior, our source. In John 15:5 (TPT), Jesus said, "I am the sprouting vine and you're My branches. As you live in union with Me as your source, fruitfulness will stream from within you—but when you live separated from Me you are powerless." That union is where healing lives. It's not something we chase. It's something that flows from staying connected to the Vine.

I've experienced this firsthand. There was a season when instead of striving to be healed, I just turned my heart toward the Lord. I would sometimes put on worship, or just sit with Him, and let His presence wash over me. No agendas. No formulas. Just time with Jesus. And in those quiet places, healing began to rise in me. Peace came. Strength returned. Pain diminished. My soul found rest—and from that place, healing began to manifest.

We often think healing comes from doing more—more declarations, more laying on of hands, more warfare. And while those things have their place, they're not the source. The source is Him. When you sit with Jesus and let His Word speak louder than your symptoms, something shifts. You begin to see yourself through His eyes—whole, loved, and full of life. That's when fear starts to lose its grip. That's when striving starts to fall off. That's when healing becomes real.

Healing isn't earned by effort. It's received through intimacy. The closer you walk with Him, the more you begin to live in what He's already paid for. That's why intimacy matters. It's not just a sweet bonus—it's the key to walking in sustained health and wholeness. So don't just pursue healing. Pursue the Healer. He wants to restore every part of you—your body, your heart, your memories, your mindset. And He'll do it as you rest in Him.

Declaration

Jesus, You are my healer and my closest friend. I receive healing not through striving, but through intimacy. I draw near to You and trust that as I abide in You, wholeness flows through me. My body, mind, and soul are being renewed in Your presence.

Father, I come close. Not with demands, but with hunger. I want You more than anything. I want to be whole in every way—not just physically, but emotionally and spiritually. I rest in Your love. I receive Your peace. Heal every part of me as I abide in You. In Jesus' name, amen.

Healing Flows

HEALING IN THE SOUL AND BODY

When we talk about healing, most people think of the physical—aches, diseases, injuries, symptoms. But God's heart is so much bigger than just the body. He doesn't want to simply relieve pain; He wants to restore wholeness. And true wholeness includes the soul—your mind, your will, your emotions. Because many times, the pain in our body is rooted in pain from the past.

God created us as three-part beings—spirit, soul, and body. And what touches one part often affects the others. You can carry stress, trauma, grief, or bitterness for years without realizing how deeply it's influencing your physical health. But here's the good news: Jesus came to heal every part of you.

3 John 1:2 (AMP) says, "Beloved, I pray that in every way you may succeed and prosper and be in good health [physically], just as [I know] your soul prospers [spiritually]." Do you catch that connection? The prosperity of the soul and the health of the body are linked.

So what does it mean for your soul to prosper? It means freedom from torment. It means peace in your thoughts, confidence in your identity, rest from fear, and joy that can't be shaken. A prospering soul is a soul that has encountered the love of God and believed it to be true. And from that place, healing flows into every other part of your being.

Many people have physical conditions that never seem to lift—chronic pain, immune disorders, tension headaches, digestive issues—and the root is something much deeper than what's visible. It could be Unprocessed Grief. Lingering Unforgiveness. Trauma that was never talked about. Constant Anxiety. Self-Hatred. These aren't just emotional battles. They're open doors that affect the body. But Jesus came to shut every one of those doors.

Luke 4:18 (TPT) reveals His mission: "The Spirit of the Lord is upon me, and He has anointed Me to be hope for the poor, healing for the brokenhearted, and new eyes for the blind, and to preach to prisoners, 'You are set free!' I have come to share the message of Jubilee, for the time of God's great acceptance has begun." He came to bind up broken hearts—not just heal blind eyes. The broken heart matters to Him just as much as the broken bone. And healing in the soul can be just as miraculous—and just as necessary—as healing in the body.

I've prayed for people who couldn't sleep, and the moment they forgave someone from their past, peace came. I've watched anxiety flee when someone renounced lies they'd believed about themselves since childhood. I've seen people delivered from torment the moment they encountered the love of God on a personal level. The freedom didn't just change their heart—it changed their health.

You don't need to be ashamed of soul pain. Jesus understands it intimately. He was "a man of sorrows, acquainted with grief" (Isaiah 53:3). He weeps with those who weep. He carries our burdens. He knows how to touch the wounded places we've hidden away for too long. Sometimes healing starts when we finally open up and say, "Lord, this hurt me. This scared me. This broke something inside me." That honesty is where His power meets your pain.

Psalm 34:18 (TPT) promises, "The Lord is close to all whose hearts are crushed by pain, and He is always ready to restore the repentant one." You don't have to hide your emotions to be full of faith. Bringing your emotions into the light is part of your faith. And as you do, God begins to work—not just on your physical symptoms, but on the deeper roots.

So if you've been contending for physical healing and haven't seen it yet, ask Holy Spirit: "Is there something deeper You want to heal?" "Is there a lie I've believed?" "Is there someone I need to forgive?" "Is there trauma You want to touch?" He's gentle. He won't overwhelm you. But He will lead you into truth. And that truth will set you free—spirit, soul, and body. When Jesus healed, He often spoke directly to the deeper issue. He told the paralytic, "Your sins are forgiven." He looked at the woman at the well and called out her shame. He wasn't interested in quick fixes—He came to make people whole. And He wants to do the same for you.

Healing in the soul can look like:

- Finally forgiving someone who deeply hurt you.

- Breaking agreement with shame or condemnation.

- Replacing lies with truth through Scripture.

- Letting go of perfectionism or fear.

- Inviting Jesus into memories where you were wounded.

And when the soul heals, the body follows.

Wholeness isn't just about pain leaving your body. It's about walking in freedom—free from torment, fear, shame, stress, and the weight of things you were never meant to carry. Jesus is still saying, "Come to Me, all who are weary and burdened, and I will give you rest." (Matthew 11:28).

Let Him restore your soul. Let Him bring peace to your emotions. Let Him break the cycles that have tried to stay for too long. This is your portion: healing in the soul and the body.

Declaration

Jesus, You came to heal every part of me—body, soul, and spirit. I open up the places in my heart that have been wounded or hidden. I receive Your peace. I let go of fear, grief, shame, and trauma. My soul is prospering, and so is my body. I am being made whole in Your love.

Prayer

Father, I invite You into every corner of my life. Not just the parts I show others—but the ones I've kept tucked away. Heal my soul. Heal my memories. Heal my mind and my emotions. And let that healing flow through every cell of my body. I thank You that You don't just want me pain-free—you want me whole. I receive that now, in Jesus' name. Amen.

Healing Flows

CHAPTER 16

PRACTICAL PATHWAYS TO RECEIVE

Sometimes healing can feel like a mystery. We know it's God's will. We believe in the finished work of the cross. We've seen others healed. But when it comes to receiving healing for ourselves, it can feel... complicated. Like we're missing a step or doing something wrong.

The truth is, receiving healing isn't about finding the right formula. It's about learning to lean into the simplicity of what God has already made available. Healing doesn't come by striving—it comes by surrender. And two of the most powerful, yet often overlooked, pathways to receiving are prayer and rest.

Prayer is more than just asking. It's communion. It's union with the heart of God. It's where we align ourselves with His truth, surrender our burdens, and listen for His voice. Prayer isn't about convincing God to heal us. It's about coming close to the One who already has. James 5:16 (AMP) says, "...The heartfelt and persistent prayer of a righteous man (believer) can accomplish much [when put into action and made effective by God—it is dynamic and can have tremendous power]." There's power in prayer—not because of our words, but because of the One we're speaking to.

Jesus modeled this perfectly. Over and over, He went away to pray. Not just to make requests, but to be with the Father. And from that place of intimacy, power flowed. When we pray, we're not just calling on a distant God. We're communing with our healer, our redeemer, our friend.

Romans 8:26 (TPT) reminds us, "And in a similar way, Holy Spirit takes hold of us in our human frailty to empower us in our weakness... at times we don't even know how to pray... But Holy Spirit rises up within us to super-intercede on our behalf, pleading to God with emotional sighs too deep for words." You don't need perfect prayers to receive healing. You just need surrendered ones.

When you pray, invite Holy Spirit to lead. Ask Him what to say, what to release, what to receive. Let Him guide your heart into the truths of the Word. Let Him reveal any lies you've believed, any fear you need to let go of, any area where you're holding on instead of resting. Rest isn't passive. It's powerful. It's not inactivity—it's spirit-led confidence that God is working even when you can't see it. In a world that says, "Do more," God says, "Be still."

Hebrews 4:10 (AMP) tells us, "For the one who has once entered His rest has also rested from [the weariness and pain of] his [human] labors, just as God rested from [thise labors uniquely] His own." Rest is a statement of faith. It says, "I trust You enough to stop striving. I believe You're good enough to finish what You started. I know healing isn't something I have to earn—it's something I get to receive."

In Exodus 14:14, as the Israelites stood trapped between Pharaoh's army and the Red Sea, Moses said, "The Lord will fight for you; you need only to be still." Stillness is not weakness. It's faith in motion. It's choosing to lie down in the green pastures while the Shepherd restores your soul (Psalm 23:1–3). It's trusting that even while you sleep, heaven is moving on your behalf.

Isaiah 30:15 (AMP) says, "In returning [to Me] and rest you shall be saved, in quietness and confident trust is your strength." Rest is strength. And rest is the atmosphere where healing thrives.

Begin and end each day with this simple prayer: "Jesus, I trust You. I rest in Your finished work. I receive healing as a gift, not a reward. Teach me to abide in You." When symptoms come, don't panic. Go back to rest. Go back to prayer. Go back to His presence.

You can also speak Scripture aloud daily—verses like:

- "By His wounds I am healed." (Isaiah 53:5)

- "The Lord is restoring health to me and healing me of all wounds." (Jeremiah 30:17)

- "I am prospering and in health even as my soul prospers." (3 John 1:2)

Speak them not to twist God's arm—but to train your heart to believe what's already true.

Declaration

Jesus, I receive healing as part of Your finished work. I lay down striving and choose to rest. I trust that You are faithful and that Your Word is true. Healing is flowing through my body right now—not because I earned it, but because You gave it. I rest, and I receive.

Prayer

Father, thank You for the gift of healing. Thank You that I don't have to fight for what Jesus already won. Teach me to pray from intimacy and rest from faith. Let Your peace rule in my heart, and let healing rise in my body. I trust You deeply. I rest in You completely. In Jesus' name, amen.

Healing Flows

CHAPTER 17

Ministering While Needing Healing

This chapter is for the ones who are still waiting. The ones still contending for healing in their own bodies while their hearts burn to see others made whole. It's for those who love to minister, who know God heals, who believe the Word is true, but who wake up some days with pain still lingering, symptoms still present, or doctors' reports still hanging in the air.

If that's you, I want you to hear this clearly: You don't need to be fully healed to be fully available. You don't have to wait until your body is perfect before you let healing flow through your hands. It may feel counterintuitive, but it's true—you can minister healing to others even while you are still in the process of receiving it yourself.

Jesus never asked for perfection before participation. He called the weak, the learning, the growing—and empowered them to move in faith. Your experience may still be unfolding, but the authority Jesus gave you is already complete.

Faith Isn't Based on Your Feelings—It's Based on His Finished Work — 2 Corinthians 4:7 (TPT) says, "We are like common clay jars that carry this glorious treasure within, so that the immeasurable power will be seen as God's, not ours." This truth frees us. We are not the source of healing—He is. And because the power is His, we don't have to feel perfect to release it. We just have to believe — IN HIM —.

I remember when I was diagnosed with spinal cord compression. The severity of it threatened paralysis if left untreated. The weight of that diagnosis was real, and it would've been easy—reasonable even—to hit pause on ministry. But the Lord never told me to stop. In fact, the opposite happened. I felt the urgency to keep pouring out, to keep laying hands on the sick, to keep declaring His Word as true. For over a year after that diagnosis, I ministered healing to others—many with issues just like mine. Slipped discs. Nerve damage. Spinal misalignments. And I watched, again and again, as the power of God moved. People were healed. Pain disappeared. Function returned. Not because I was at 100%, but because the Spirit within me was.

Eventually, I did go through surgery. I'm still walking out full restoration in my own body. But nothing has stopped healing from flowing through me. If anything, the compassion and hunger to see others healed has only deepened. Because I know what it's like to stand in the tension—to feel pain and still speak healing. To wrestle through the night and still rise up and declare, "Jesus is Healer."

Ministering from the Middle

You don't have to have your breakthrough before you can release breakthrough. Some of the most powerful moments of ministry happen while we're still "in the middle." That's because when we minister from that place, it's raw. It's real.

It's faith that has nothing to lean on but the Word of God. And that kind of faith moves heaven. Romans 4:20–21 (AMP) speaks of Abraham's example: "But he did not doubt or waver in unbelief concerning the promise of God, but he grew strong and empowered by faith, giving glory to God, being fully convinced that God had the power to do what He had promised." Abraham didn't wait until the promise manifested before he gave glory to God. He praised and believed while still childless. And God called that faith righteous.

The same is true for us. There is a righteousness, a glory, and a boldness that comes when we declare healing over someone else while we ourselves are still walking through it. You are not being fake when you do this. You are being faithful.

Pastor John Anosike: A Testimony of Faithful Ministry

One incredible example of this is Pastor John Anosike. While ministering healing to thousands—miracle after miracle, testimony after testimony—he himself was carrying a heart condition so severe, doctors said it would take his life within two years. Yet, he did not quit. He kept standing. He kept declaring. He kept ministering. And the miracles didn't stop. In fact, they increased. Because healing isn't about the vessel—it's about the power that flows through the vessel. Listen to this again—Healing isn't about the vessel—it's about the power that flows through the vessel. Remember that!

There's something powerful about ministering from your weakness. It exposes the lie that healing is about spiritual elitism. It crushes the idea that only the "fully fixed" get to minister. No—it's about Jesus, and He chooses to use the willing, not only the well.

You Are Still Anointed—filled with His Holy Spirit. You are still commissioned to heal the sick. You are still a carrier of the Kingdom. Your authority has not been revoked just because you're in process. Luke 10:19 (AMP) says, "Listen carefully: I have given you authority [that you now possess] to tread on serpents and scorpions, and [the ability to exercise authority] over all the power of the enemy (Satan); and nothing will [in any way] harm you."

That verse didn't come with fine print. It didn't say "only on days when you feel good" or "only if your own body is fully healed." It says—you now possess authority. So walk in it. Use it. Pray with confidence. Lay hands with boldness. You may be ministering while needing healing yourself—but heaven is backing you.

Often, as you give, you begin to receive. The very river you pour out of becomes the stream you drink from. Because when you move in obedience, you create space for the power of God to move through and around you.

Declaration

I am anointed to heal, even as I walk through my own healing. Jesus is my source. The Spirit within me is not limited by my experience. I walk in boldness and obedience. Healing flows through my hands, because the power is His. I minister from faith, not from feelings—and I will see miracles in others and in myself.

Prayer

Father, thank You that I don't have to be perfect to be powerful in Your hands. Thank You that healing flows because of Jesus—not because of me. I trust You with my process, and I trust You to move through me as I minister. Strengthen my heart. Let compassion rise. Let faith increase. Use me to heal the sick, even as You heal me. In Jesus' name, amen.

Healing Flows

CHAPTER 18

OVERFLOW – HEALING OTHERS FROM A HEALED IDENTITY

There was a season about 18 or 20 months ago when I began to truly rest daily in the presence of God. Not with an agenda, not looking for a particular outcome—just being with Him. Early in the morning, sometimes with worship playing quietly in the background, sometimes reading The Word, other times just sitting in the stillness, I purposed my heart to be with Him—and something began to shift. I started noticing that healing flowed more naturally when I prayed for others. It wasn't because I was trying harder or praying longer—it was because I was resting in Him. From that place, I could hear His voice more clearly. I felt His nudge more easily. I wasn't guessing when to move, when to wait, or what to say. There was clarity. There was confidence. There was flow.

I realized then what I've carried into every part of ministry since: healing flows best from identity, not effort. The power to heal doesn't come from working yourself into a spiritual frenzy—it comes from abiding. It's the fruit of knowing who you are and Whose you are.

The moment we gave our lives to Jesus, we were made new—completely. Spiritually whole. Seated with Him. Healed in the eyes of heaven. Colossians 2:10 (AMP) says, "And in Him you have been made complete [achieving spiritual stature through Christ]." You don't have to strive for wholeness when you've already been made whole in Him. The healed identity you carry in your spirit is already true—it just needs to be believed and lived from.

Healing, in that sense, becomes the overflow of a person who is rooted in truth. John 15:5 (TPT) says, "I am the sprouting vine and you're My branches. As you live in union with Me as your source, fruitfulness will stream from within you—but when you live separated from Me you are powerless." That fruit includes healing. It flows from union, not pressure. From rest, not religious hustle.

I'm not saying you won't feel resistance. There are moments when it would be easier to shift into old habits—trying to say just the right words, praying longer, pushing harder, even quoting scripture that you have knowledge of. But I've found that the more I rest in Him, the more the Spirit does the work. In that season of rest I mentioned, I stopped trying to make things happen. I started showing up in peace, listening more, speaking less, and watching Holy Spirit do more with a few words of obedience than I ever could with a well-crafted scripture-filled prayer that I composed from my educated carnal mind. Healing became effortless—not because I had grown in skill, but because I had grown in surrender.

Galatians 2:20 (TPT) says, "My old identity has been co-crucified with Messiah and no longer lives… the essence of this new life is no longer mine, for the Anointed One lives His life through me—we live in union as one!" That's not just a nice verse—it's our blueprint for ministry. When Jesus is living through you, healing flows without striving. It's not a matter of working yourself up—it's about showing up as who you already are: His.

When you pray for someone, you're not trying to manufacture a miracle—you're releasing what already lives in you. You're not begging heaven to open—you're realizing heaven already moved in. Instead of pleading, "Lord, use me," begin to declare, "Thank You, Jesus, that healing flows from me because I'm one with You." You're not trying to build up to power—you're walking in it. You're not waiting for a feeling—you're operating from a reality.

That's what it means to minister from a healed identity. You stop chasing a result and start living from revelation. You stop worrying about outcomes and start trusting the presence. You let go of the pressure to perform and embrace the joy of simply releasing what's already inside. Isaiah 30:15 (AMP) says, "In returning [to Me] and rest you shall be saved, in quietness and confident trust is your strength." Real authority comes in quiet confidence. Healing doesn't require hype. It requires surrender.

When you minister from identity, you start to see others differently. You don't just see their pain or diagnosis—you see their inheritance. You see them as sons and daughters of a Father who already paid for their healing. You speak to their bodies from that place of spiritual clarity, knowing that you're not trying to convince God to do something. You're simply releasing what Jesus already purchased.

You're not ministering for identity—you're ministering from it. You don't heal to prove anything. You heal because it's who you are. And when you know that, there's no pressure. There's just overflow.

Declaration

I am one with Christ. His life flows through me. I minister healing from my true identity—not from fear, pressure, or striving. I rest in who He is and who He has made me to be. I am healed, I am whole, and healing flows through me effortlessly because I am abiding in the Vine.

Prayer

Jesus, thank You that I don't have to perform to be powerful. Thank You that You live in me and healing flows through me. Teach me to live in rest. Help me stay connected to You, to hear Your voice, to walk in confidence. Let healing be the fruit of intimacy, not effort. I receive Your peace and I move in Your power. In Your name, amen.

Healing Flows

CHAPTER 19

COMMUNITY AND HEALING

Healing was never meant to be a solo journey. God designed the Church to be a body, not just individuals walking alone with Jesus. There's something powerful, even sacred, about pursuing healing together—in faith, in unity, and in the context of spiritual family. Sometimes we're tempted to isolate when we're hurting. Pain makes us want to retreat, pull back, and "just deal with it ourselves." But that's not how healing was meant to work. God often uses the very people around you—your community, family, and friends.

When we come together in unity, we create an atmosphere where Holy Spirit loves to move. In Matthew 18:20 (AMP), Jesus said, "For where two or three are gathered in My name [meeting together as My followers], I am there among them." The presence of Jesus becomes tangible when we gather around His name. That's not poetic—it's powerful. Healing shows up when Jesus is at the center. And often, that happens in community.

I've seen it. There's a difference in the atmosphere when believers come into agreement—when hearts are united in love, when compassion flows, when nobody's trying to prove anything, just simply leaning into the goodness of God together. That's when healing breaks out. Sometimes it's in a church service during worship. Sometimes it's around a dinner table. Sometimes it's on a sidewalk, with hands stretched out in faith. It doesn't matter where—what matters is that we're together and He's in our midst.

Acts 2:42–43 (AMP) gives us a picture of the early Church: "They were continually and faithfully devoting themselves to the instruction of the apostles, and to fellowship, to eating meals together and to prayers. A sense of awe was felt by everyone, and many wonders and signs (attesting miracles) were taking place through the apostles." Healing was normal. Miracles happened in the context of fellowship. They weren't just attending services—they were doing life together. That unity created a climate where the presence and power of God flowed freely. That unity created a climate where faith was alive, where love was expressed in action, and where the supernatural wasn't rare — it was expected. They weren't striving for miracles — they were walking in relationship with the Miracle Worker. Healing didn't flow from special events — it flowed from a lifestyle of connection to Jesus and connection to one another. The early Church wasn't built on polished sermons or programs — it was built on surrendered hearts, devoted prayer, real community, and the living power of God at work among them daily.

That's still His design today. Healing flows in the atmosphere of unity, love, and faith-filled expectation. Where Jesus is truly the center—miracles follow naturally.

And here's what's beautiful: you don't have to be in a packed church with a healing evangelist to experience this. You only need people who believe. People who know who they are in Christ and who He is in them. People who carry the same Spirit. That's what activates the healing atmosphere. It's not about how big the crowd is—it's about the agreement in the room. One person within your group, obeying Christ and believing in Him is enough.

James 5:16 (AMP) says, "Confess your sins to one another [your false steps, your offenses], and pray for one another, that you may be healed and restored. The heartfelt and persistent prayer of a righteous man (believer) can accomplish much." There's healing in vulnerability. Healing in prayer. Healing in humility. When we walk in the light together, healing flows more freely.

Some of the most powerful healing moments I've witnessed happened not on stages but in Retail stores, small group gatherings, small family gatherings in living rooms, motel lobbies, and during quiet ministry moments at the back or side of the church when no one else was watching. Why? Because Jesus was there. Faith was present. And hearts were open.

And it goes both ways. There will be times when you're the one who needs community to carry you. Just like the paralyzed man in Luke 5 whose friends broke through the roof to get him to Jesus, you need people in your life who will carry you when you can't walk on your own. And there will be times when you're that person for someone else. This is the beauty of the body of Christ. We're not competing—we're completing. We each bring our portion. And when those portions come together in unity, miracles happen.

We need each other. You were never meant to "figure out" healing on your own. God has placed you in a body for a reason. And there's something about agreeing in faith together, declaring the Word together, laying hands together—that amplifies what God is doing. You can absolutely receive healing on your own—but God also loves to move through the family. It's His nature. He's a relational God. And He heals through relationship.

So lean into community. Don't retreat. Don't isolate. Whether you feel strong or weak, show up. Bring your faith, bring your expectation, bring your vulnerability. Watch what happens when you do. Healing flows through unity. It flows through fellowship. It flows through love.

Declaration

I am part of the body of Christ. I was made for community. Healing flows in the atmosphere of unity, faith, and love. I will not isolate—I will lean in. God uses people to release His power, and I receive and release healing in the context of His family. I am covered, connected, and called to bring life wherever I go.

Prayer

Father, thank You for placing me in Your body. Thank You for brothers and sisters who carry faith, love, and strength. Help me to stay connected—to show up, to be real, and to believe with others. Let healing flow in my relationships. Let community become a place of miracles. Use me to lift others up and let others lift me when I need it. I welcome the healing that comes through family. In Jesus' name, amen.

Healing Flows

CHAPTER 20

LIVING A LIFESTYLE OF HEALING

Healing is not meant to be a moment—it's meant to be a way of life. It's not just something we receive when we're sick or something we minister when the setting is right. It's a continual, daily flow of life from heaven to earth, from God's Spirit through your spirit, into your body, and out through your hands to touch the world around you.

Living a lifestyle of healing means we don't clock in and clock out of being vessels for the miraculous. It means we're always available, always listening, always carrying the presence of the One who heals. The same Spirit who raised Jesus from the dead lives in you (Romans 8:11). That Spirit doesn't take days off. And neither does your assignment.

There's something powerful that happens when you shift your mindset from "occasionally being used" to "constantly being available." When healing becomes your default, not your exception, you start to realize the world around you is full of divine opportunities. People are everywhere. Pain is everywhere. But more importantly, Jesus is everywhere—and He lives in you.

So here's what I want to encourage you with as we close this book: start paying attention everywhere you go. Whether you're at a gas station, a grocery store, a restaurant, or on a walk—there is always someone God wants to minister to. Healing flows best through people who are paying attention. If you'll stay available, God will use you.

You don't need a word of knowledge every time. You don't need thunder from heaven. You just need to obey the whisper. Sometimes it's as simple as, "Ask if they're in pain." Or, "Offer to pray." And when you do—when you say yes in that moment—the power of God flows. Not because of your perfection, but because of your obedience.

Mark 16:17–18 (AMP) gives us our marching orders: "These signs will accompany those who have believed: in My name they will cast out demons, they will speak in new tongues… they will lay hands on the sick, and they will get well." That's not reserved for the platform. That's meant for the parking lot, the workplace, the bus stop, and the coffee shop. It's for every believer—which means it's for you.

You are a walking, breathing conduit of heaven. Every room you walk into shifts because the Healer just entered. Every space becomes a sanctuary. Every hand you extend becomes a highway for the anointing. When you begin to live with that kind of awareness, healing doesn't stay rare—it becomes normal.

Matthew 10:7–8 (TPT) says, "As you go, preach this message: 'Heaven's kingdom realm is accessible, close enough to touch!' You must continually bring healing to lepers and to those who are sick, and make it your habit to break off the demonic presence from people…" As you go. That's the key. Not just when you're in church. Not just when you're invited to pray.

As you go. Healing is part of your daily rhythm. It's your lifestyle.

And here's the beauty: as you live this lifestyle of healing, you're not just helping others—you're reinforcing your own wholeness. When healing flows through you, it strengthens what's happening in you. The more you give, the more you walk in it. The more you pour out, the more heaven pours in.

So wake up every day with this simple prayer: "Lord, who do You want to touch through me today?" And then go. Live. Be you. But be alert. You'll start noticing the limps, the bandages, the tension in shoulders, the tiredness in eyes. And when you do, be bold. Extend your hand. Speak the name of Jesus. Release healing. You carry the answer inside you.

Healing is not reserved for the elite. It's not boxed into services or conferences. It's in your living room. It's in your hallway. It's in your phone call. It's in your hands. You are not waiting for another anointing—you are already anointed. The Spirit of the Lord is upon you.

So live this thing. Let it get into your bones. Let healing become part of your personality. Let it be normal. Expected. Constant. Whether you feel on fire or not. Whether you've seen results lately or not. You're not living for results—you're living from truth.

You were made to release the life of heaven. Every day. Everywhere you go. To everyone who will receive.

Declaration

Healing is my lifestyle. I walk in divine health and I release it everywhere I go. I pay attention to the nudges of Holy Spirit. I carry the answer inside me. I am bold, available, and obedient. I live in union with the Healer, and healing flows through my hands every day.

Father, thank You for trusting me with Your power. Thank You that healing isn't something I have to force—it's something I live in. Make me more aware. Help me see the people around me the way You do. I say yes to Your promptings. I choose to live with open eyes, open hands, and a heart that burns to release Your love. Use me, Lord. I am Yours. In Jesus' name, amen.

Healing Flows

Conclusion

The same Jesus who walked the streets of Galilee healing the sick is still alive. Still present. Still moving through His people.

Healing was never meant to stay locked in the pages of a book — even this book. Healing flows because Jesus still lives. Healing flows because the Spirit of God still empowers believers today to do what He said we would do.

This isn't about chasing experiences or striving for miracles. It's about walking with the Healer — living close, listening well, loving boldly, and obeying quickly.

Healing flows through everyday people who simply believe God means what He says. Healing flows through quiet prayers in living rooms. It flows in grocery stores and job sites. It flows in hospitals and on back porches. Healing flows through sons and daughters who know who their Father is — and are willing to step out.

Don't complicate it. Don't wait until you feel ready. Don't wait until everything in your own life looks perfect.

If you belong to Jesus — healing flows. It flows through you when you lay hands on the sick. It flows through you when you speak His Word. It flows when you show up in love, stand in faith, and trust that the power isn't in your ability — it's in His finished work. Stay connected to Him. Stay in the Word. Stay available. Because healing still flows. And He wants it to flow through you.

Call to Salvation

The greatest healing you'll ever receive is not physical — it's spiritual. It's the healing of your heart. The forgiveness of sin. The restoration of relationship between you and God. That's why Jesus came.

If you've never surrendered your life to Him — or if you know it's time to come home — this is your moment.

Salvation isn't about religion. It's not about joining a church or trying to be good enough. It's about trusting Jesus — the One who loves you, died for you, and rose again to give you life. Romans 10:9 says, "If you declare with your mouth, 'Jesus is Lord,' and believe in your heart that God raised him from the dead, you will be saved." That's for you. Right here. Right now.

If you're ready to make that decision, pray this from your heart:

Jesus, I believe You are the Son of God. I believe You died for me. I believe You rose again. And today — I surrender. I give You my heart. I give You my life. I turn from my sin, and I turn fully to You. Forgive me. Wash me clean. Heal every part of me. Fill me with Your Holy Spirit. Lead me from this day forward. I want to follow You — fully and forever. Thank You for saving me. Thank You for loving me. Amen.

Scripture Index

Old Testament

- Exodus 15:26 – God reveals Himself as Healer (Chapter 1)

- Psalm 103:2–3 – He forgives all sin and heals all disease (Chapters 1, 14)

- Psalm 105:37 – Not one feeble among them (Chapter 1)

- Isaiah 53:4–5 – By His wounds we are healed (Chapters 2, 11)

- Isaiah 11:2 – Spirit of wisdom and understanding (Chapter 8)

- Isaiah 30:15 – Quietness and confident trust is your strength (Chapters 16, 18)

- Psalm 34:18 – The Lord is close to the brokenhearted (Chapter 15)

- Exodus 14:14 – The Lord will fight for you (Chapter 16)

Gospels

- Matthew 8:3 – "I am willing, be cleansed." (Chapters 1, 9)

- Matthew 8:16–17 – He took our sickness and removed our diseases (Chapters 1, 2)

- Matthew 10:8 – The Commission (Chapters 5, 7, 20)

- Matthew 10:7–8 – The Kingdom is near; bring healing (Chapter 20)

- Matthew 16:18 – Lay hands on the sick and they will recover (Chapters 5, 10, 20)

- Mark 5:28 – "If I just touch His clothes…" (Chapter 4)
- Mark 5:34 – "Your faith has made you well." (Chapters 4, 11)
- Mark 6:5 – He laid hands on a few and healed them (Chapter 5)
- Mark 8:22–25 – Partial healing, then full sight (Chapters 7, 9)
- Luke 4:18 – Anointed to bring healing (Chapters 3, 15)
- Luke 4:40 – He laid hands on each one and healed them (Chapter 5)
- Luke 5 – Forgiveness before physical healing (Chapters 8, 19)
- Luke 8:48 – "Daughter, your faith has healed you." (Chapter 14)
- Luke 9:1–2 – He gave them power and authority (Chapter 5)
- Luke 10:19 – Authority over all the power of the enemy (Chapters 6, 17)
- John 5:19 – The Son does what He sees the Father doing (Chapters 1, 8)
- John 7:38–39 – Rivers of living water will flow (Chapter 6)
- John 14:16–17 – Holy Spirit is with you forever (Chapter 3)
- John 15:5 – Abide in Me and bear fruit (Chapters 14, 18)

Acts & Epistles

- Acts 3:6 – "In the name of Jesus, walk!" (Chapters 5, 7)
- Acts 9:17–18 – Ananias lays hands and Saul regains sight (Chapter 5)
- Acts 10:38 – Jesus healed all (Chapters 1, 3)

- Acts 2:42–43 – Signs and wonders (Chapter 19)
- Romans 4:20–21 – Abraham did not waver (Chapter 17)
- Romans 8:11 – Life to your mortal bodies by the Spirit (Chapters 3, 12, 20)
- Romans 10:17 – Faith comes by hearing the message of Christ (Chapter 4)
- Romans 12:2 – Be transformed by renewing your mind (Chapter 11)
- Romans 1:11 – Longing to impart spiritual gifts (Chapter 6)
- 2 Corinthians 4:7 – Treasure in jars of clay (Chapter 17)
- 2 Corinthians 5:17 – You are a new creation (Chapter 12)
- Galatians 2:20 – Christ lives in me (Chapters 12, 18)
- Ephesians 2:6 – Seated with Christ in heavenly places (Chapter 12)
- Ephesians 2:8 – By grace you have been saved through faith (Chapter 4)
- Ephesians 6:13 – Stand firm after doing all (Chapter 4)
- Philippians 1:6 – He completes what He starts (Chapter 9)
- Colossians 2:10 – You have been made complete in Christ (Chapter 18)
- Colossians 2:14–15 – He canceled the legal demands against us (Chapter 2)
- Hebrews 4:10 – Resting from our works (Chapter 16)

- Hebrews 6:12 – Through faith and patience inherit the promise (Chapter 9)

- Hebrews 10:23 – Hold tightly to hope (Chapter 10)

- Hebrews 10:35–36 – Don't throw away your confidence (Chapter 13)

- James 1:6–8 – Ask without doubting (Chapters 11, 13)

- James 5:15–16 – Prayer of faith will restore the sick (Chapters 4, 16, 19)

- 1 Peter 2:24 – By His wounds you were healed (Chapter 2)

- 1 Timothy 5:23 – Use a little wine (Chapter 10)

- 2 Timothy 1:6 – Fan into flame the gift through laying on of hands (Chapter 5)

- 2 Timothy 4:20 – Paul left Trophimus sick (Chapter 10)

- 3 John 1:2 – Health as your soul prospers (Chapters 15, 16)

Identity Scriptures for Bold Faith & Healing

New Creation Realities / Identity

2 Corinthians 5:17 - *"Therefore if any man be in Christ, he is a new creature: old things are passed away; behold, all things are become new."*

John 1:12 - *"But as many as received him, to them gave he power to become the sons of God, even to them that believe on his name."*

1 John 4:4 - *"Greater is he that is in you, than he that is in the world."*

Righteousness & Redemption

2 Corinthians 5:21 - *"For he hath made him to be sin for us, who knew no sin; that we might be made the righteousness of God in him."*

Galatians 3:13 - *"Christ hath redeemed us from the curse of the law, being made a curse for us..."*

Romans 8:1 - *"There is therefore now no condemnation to them which are in Christ Jesus..."*

Authority & Power in the Name of Jesus

John 14:13-14 - *"And whatsoever ye shall ask in my name, that will I do..."*

Mark 16:17-18 - *"In my name shall they cast out devils; they shall speak with new tongues... they shall lay hands on the sick, and they shall recover."*

Philippians 2:9-10 - "*Wherefore God also hath highly exalted him, and given him a name which is above every name...*"

The Power of Words / Confession

Mark 11:23-24 - "*He shall have whatsoever he saith...*"

Proverbs 18:21 - "*Death and life are in the power of the tongue...*"

Hebrews 10:23 - "*Let us hold fast the profession (confession) of our faith without wavering...*"

Healing & God's Will to Heal

Isaiah 53:4-5 - "*By his stripes we are healed.*"

Matthew 8:17 - "*Himself took our infirmities, and bare our sicknesses.*"

1 Peter 2:24 - "*By whose stripes ye were healed.*"

Epilogue

If I could sit across the table from you right now, I'd probably say something like this...

Thank you for caring enough about the heart of God to read a book like this.

I don't have all the answers. I never have. But I've seen enough of Jesus to know He's everything He says He is. He still heals. He still saves. He still uses regular, imperfect people to do things we could never do on our own.

I'm still learning. Still growing. Still believing for my own breakthroughs while watching Him work through my hands for others. That's the mystery and beauty of walking with Him.

Healing flows because He flows. And He's not finished with you. This isn't the end of the story. This is the beginning of a new one. Stay in His presence. Stay in His Word. Stay in step with Holy Spirit.

There are people waiting on the other side of your obedience. There are hearts waiting to be loved. Bodies waiting to be healed. Lives waiting to encounter Jesus in a way they never have before.

And He's chosen you. So let's keep going.
Let's keep laying hands on the sick.
Let's keep declaring His promises.
Let's keep showing up in love and letting healing flow.
Not because we're special — Because He is.

Prayer of Blessing over you:

Father, I thank You for every person reading this. You know them by name. You see every need, every heartache, every desire, and every hope. I speak blessing over them in Jesus' name. I declare healing over their body, their mind, and their heart. I ask You, Holy Spirit, to lead them into truth, to fill them with Your power, and to flow through their life in ways they never imagined. Let them be carriers of Your love. Let them be bold with Your Word. Let them walk in peace, in joy, and in unshakable confidence that You are with them. Heal them. Use them. Lead them. And may healing flow through their life everywhere they go — all for Your glory, Jesus.

Amen.

About the Author

Timothy H. Linn is an ordinary guy following an extraordinary God.

For nearly 30 years, he worked as a home builder and a flat work concrete contractor — hands in the dirt, early mornings, deadlines. But along the way, Jesus captured his heart in a way that is now changing everything.

Tim is an outdoorsman at heart — he loves to hunt, fish, and spend time in God's creation. He's just as comfortable on a mountain or a back road as he is anywhere. But no matter where life takes him, his greatest passion is seeing people encounter the real Jesus — the Jesus who still heals, still speaks, and still moves in power today.

He doesn't come from a stage or a spotlight. He comes from job sites, ordinary days, and a life that's been marked by the faithfulness of God. Tim believes healing is for today — and it's for everyone. He believes every believer is called to walk in sonship, live in intimacy with the Father, and let healing flow through their lives in practical, real ways. He's not writing books to build a platform. He's writing because he knows what it's like to need healing — and to see God show up again and again.

Tim's heart is simple: love Jesus, trust His Word, and help others do the same.

He continues to write, teach, and minister healing wherever God opens the door — believing that the best stories are still being written.

Healing Flows

www.ingramcontent.com/pod-product-compliance
Lightning Source LLC
Chambersburg PA
CBHW071121090426
42736CB00012B/1968